Endorsements for the Flourish Bible Study Series

"The brilliant and beautiful mix of sound teaching, helpful charts, lists, sidebars, and appealing graphics—as well as insightful questions that get the reader into the text of Scripture—make these studies that women will want to invest time in and will look back on as time well spent."

Nancy Guthrie, Bible teacher; author, *Even Better than Eden*

"My daughter and I love using Flourish Bible Studies for our morning devotions. Lydia Brownback's faithful probing of biblical texts; insightful questions; invitations to engage in personal applications using additional biblical texts and historical contexts; and commitment to upholding the whole counsel of God as it bears on living life as a godly woman has drawn us closer to the Lord and to his word. Brownback never sidesteps hard questions or hard providences, but neither does she appeal to discourses of victimhood or therapy, which are painfully common in the genre of women's Bible studies. I cannot recommend this series highly enough. My daughter and I look forward to working through this whole series together!"

Rosaria Butterfield, Former Professor of English, Syracuse University; author, *The Gospel Comes with a House Key*

"As a women's ministry leader, I am excited about the development of the Flourish Bible Study series, which will not only prayerfully equip women to increase in biblical literacy but also come alongside them to build a systematic and comprehensive framework to become lifelong students of the word of God. This series provides visually engaging studies with accessible content that will not only strengthen the believer but the church as well."

Karen Hodge, Coordinator of Women's Ministries, Presbyterian Church in America; coauthor, *Transformed*

"Lydia Brownback is an experienced Bible teacher who has dedicated her life to ministry roles that help women (and men) grow in Christ. With a wealth of biblical, historical, and theological content, her Flourish Bible Studies are ideal for groups and individuals that are serious about the in-depth study of the word of God."

Phil and Lisa Ryken, President, Wheaton College; and his wife, Lisa

"If you're looking for rich, accessible, and deeply biblical Bible studies, this series is for you! Lydia Brownback leads her readers through different books of the Bible, providing background information, maps, timelines, and questions that probe the text in order to glean understanding and application. She settles us deeply in the context of a book as she highlights God's unfolding plan of redemption and rescue. You will learn, you will delight in God's word, and you will love our good King Jesus even more."

Courtney Doctor, Coordinator of Women's Initiatives, The Gospel Coalition; author, *From Garden to Glory* and *Steadfast*

"Lydia Brownback's Bible study series provides a faithful guide to book after book. You'll find rich insights into context and good questions to help you study and interpret the Bible. Page by page, the studies point you to respond to each passage and to love our great and gracious God. I will recommend the Flourish series for years to come for those looking for a wise, Christ-centered study that leads toward the goal of being transformed by the word."

Taylor Turkington, Bible teacher; Director, BibleEquipping.org

"Lydia Brownback has a contagious love for the Bible. Not only is she fluent in the best of biblical scholarship in the last generation, but her writing is accessible to the simplest of readers. She has the rare ability of being clear without being reductionistic. I anticipate many women indeed will flourish through her trustworthy guidance in this series."

David Mathis, Senior Teacher and Executive Editor, desiringGod.org; Pastor, Cities Church, Saint Paul, Minnesota; author, *Habits of Grace*

"Lydia Brownback's Flourish Bible Study series has been a huge gift to the women's ministry in my local church. Many of our groups have gone through her studies in both the Old and New Testaments and have benefited greatly. The Flourish Bible Study series is now my go-to for a combination of rich Bible study, meaningful personal application, and practical group interaction. I recommend them whenever a partner in ministry asks me for quality women's Bible study resources. I'm so thankful Brownback continues to write them and share them with us!"

Jen Oshman, author, *Enough about Me and Cultural Counterfeits*; Women's Ministry Coordinator, Redemption Parker, Colorado

JUDGES

Flourish Bible Study Series
By Lydia Brownback

Judges: The Path from Chaos to Kingship

Esther: The Hidden Hand of God

Luke: Good News of Great Joy

1–2 Peter: Living Hope in a Hard World

FLOURISH
BIBLE STUDY

JUDGES

THE PATH FROM CHAOS TO KINGSHIP

LYDIA BROWNBACK

WHEATON, ILLINOIS

Judges: The Path from Chaos to Kingship

Copyright © 2021 by Lydia Brownback

Published by Crossway
        1300 Crescent Street
        Wheaton, Illinois 60187

Cover design: Crystal Courtney

First printing 2021

Printed in China

Scripture quotations are from the ESV® Bible (The Holy Bible, English Standard Version®), copyright © 2001 by Crossway, a publishing ministry of Good News Publishers. Used by permission. All rights reserved.

All emphases in Scripture quotations have been added by the author.

Trade paperback ISBN: 978-1-4335-6995-1

Crossway is a publishing ministry of Good News Publishers.

RRDS   34 33 32 31 30 29 28 27 26 25 24
14   13   12   11   10 9 8 7 6 5 4 3 2

With gratitude to God
for
Erika Allen,
whose gentleness, compassion, and wisdom
lift heavy hearts and reflect our Lord and Savior.

CONTENTS

THE PLACE OF JUDGES
IN BIBLICAL HISTORY

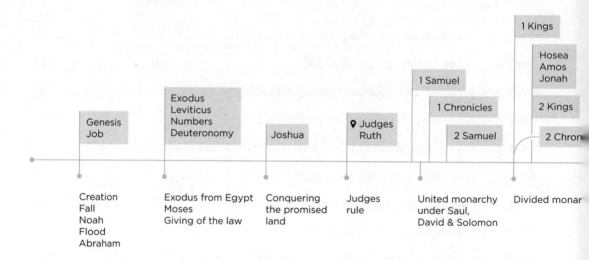

| Genesis
Job | Exodus
Leviticus
Numbers
Deuteronomy | Joshua | 📍 Judges
Ruth | 1 Samuel
1 Chronicles
2 Samuel | 1 Kings
Hosea
Amos
Jonah
2 Kings
2 Chron |

Creation
Fall
Noah
Flood
Abraham

Exodus from Egypt
Moses
Giving of the law

Conquering
the promised
land

Judges
rule

United monarchy
under Saul,
David & Solomon

Divided monar

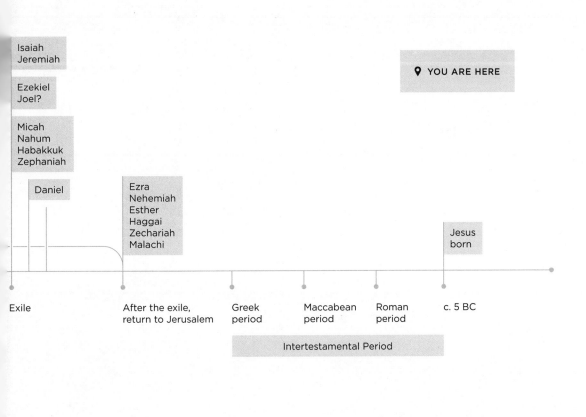

Isaiah
Jeremiah

Ezekiel
Joel?

Micah
Nahum
Habakkuk
Zephaniah

Daniel

Ezra
Nehemiah
Esther
Haggai
Zechariah
Malachi

YOU ARE HERE

Jesus
born

Exile

After the exile,
return to Jerusalem

Greek
period

Maccabean
period

Roman
period

c. 5 BC

Intertestamental Period

INTRODUCTION

GETTING INTO JUDGES

The book of Judges has all the elements of a cinematic blockbuster—intrigue, trickery, violence, murder, lust, and adultery. You name it, everything that typically leads to an R-rating (or worse) is here. And, sadly, the ones caught up in all this muck are God's very own people. We can only sit by and watch them go down, down, down. That's where the Israelites, God's people, are going, but actually they should have been going up, up, up.

Under the leadership of Joshua, the Lord had brought his people to Canaan, the promised land, and instructed them to go in and possess it. Yes, there would be enemies to fight in the process, but the Lord had promised them victory because he would be with them every step of the way. But Israel craved ease, and they found they liked the lifestyle of these Canaanite enemies, so befriending them became preferable to conquering them. That's where our story begins.

Of course, as the story progresses we're going to see that disregarding God's instructions didn't work out the way Israel hoped. Disobeying God never does, right? But the difficulties they experienced in their disobedience didn't stop their downward course. Again and again, when the Canaanite frenemies became outright enemies and therefore a dangerous threat, God's people persisted in going their own way and handling things on their own terms. Down, down, down. The Lord had every right to just stand back and let them utterly destroy themselves, but he didn't. All along he was preparing them for a greater blessing than any they'd ever known.

STARRING ROLES

We're going to encounter many intriguing people in these twenty-one chapters—so many that we'll identify just a few right here. There are, of course, the twelve judges from whom the book gets its name: Othniel, Ehud, Shamgar, Deborah (accompanied by Barak), Gideon, Tola, Jair, Jephthah,

---

Pronunciation Guide

Abimelech: a-BIM-a-lek

Adoni-bezek:
  add-Ō-nī-BEE-zick

Amalekite: am-AL-a-kite

Ammonite: AM-mon-ite

Amorite: AM-or-ite

Barak: ba-ROCK

Canaanite: KAY-na-nite

Cushan-rishathaim:
  CUSH-ann-RISH-a-THAY-um

Delilah: da-LIE-la

Eglon: EGG-lon

Ehud: EE-hood

Ephraim: EE-phree-um

Heber: HEE-bur

Hittite: HIT-ite

Hivite: HIV-ite

Jabin: JAY-bin

Jael: JAY-el

Jebusite: JEB-u-zite

Jephthah: JEFF-tha

Jerubbaal: jeroo-BAAL

Manasseh: muh-NASS-a

Manoah: man-OH-a

Naphtali: naff-TAL-ee

Othniel: OTH-nee-el

Perizzite: PEAR-a-zite

Philistine: PHIL-a-steen

Ibzan, Elon, Abdon, and Samson. Of these twelve, a few play a prominent role in the book, while others are given just a bare mention. Women play a major role, women like the riveting Jael and the manipulative Delilah, as well as several unnamed women. And making an appearance more than once is the angel of the Lord. Of course, the Lord God is actively involved in every scene, even when we aren't specifically told he's there.

SETTING

In the first book of the Bible, Genesis, God made a promise to a man named Abraham:

> I will establish my covenant between me and you and your offspring after you throughout their generations for an everlasting covenant, to be God to you and to your offspring after you. And I will give to you and to your offspring after you the land of your sojournings, all the land of Canaan, for an everlasting possession, and I will be their God. (Genesis 17:7–8)

Canaan—this land God had promised to Abraham—is the setting of our story. The Lord himself had described the land as "a good and broad land, a land flowing with milk and honey" (Exodus 3:8). You can get an idea of the size of Canaan from the map on page 16. This land is in the Middle East, and today it includes Israel, Lebanon, Jordan, Syria, and Palestine.

Joshua was the one to actually carry out God's promise to Abraham. As we noted at the beginning, Joshua brought God's people into Canaan and divided this promised land among them. Under Joshua's leadership and at the Lord's command, Israel moved in and began to displace the Canaanites who lived there. But then Joshua died, and Israel grew careless about obeying the Lord. That's where Israel is when our story begins. The events recorded in Judges cover a span just under three hundred years (1360–1084 BC), leading up to a new era in Israel's history, an era in which they will be ruled by kings rather than judges. So much happened during the time of the judges—way too much to record in a single Bible book—so the author of Judges selected particular episodes that best fit his theme. And if you know your Old Testament history, you're likely to note that he didn't record these episodes in chronological order. So, for example, the sordid stories in the final chapters likely occurred quite early in the period of the judges rather than near the end. Overall, the author arranged the material not to lay out a careful history lesson but to best show the declining spiritual condition of God's people during this three-hundred-year period.

The Judges: Servants of God

These stories are not primarily about the judges as individuals: the judges' main function is to dispense God's justice and merciful faithfulness to his people, usually by military deliverance. All servants of God's purposes for his people have their flaws; [including the judges!]. Even in these circumstances, God is working out his plan; he is not thwarted, even by human failure.[1]

In Judges the events are carefully chosen to advance the book's theological purpose, to persuade you of something. . . . The reader should let it be what it is— essentially a theological argument using patterned history as illustration.[2]

The Setting of Judges[3]

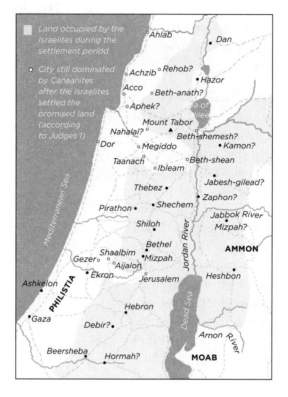

Land occupied by the
Israelites during the
settlement period

City still dominated
by Canaanites
after the Israelites
settled the
promised land
(according
to Judges 1)

Ahlab

Dan

Achzib ○ *Rehob?*

Acco ○ *Beth-anath?*

Hazor

Aphek?

*Sea of
Galilee*

Mount Tabor
Nahalal? ○   *Beth-shemesh?*
Dor   ○ *Megiddo*   *Kamon?*

Taanach   *Beth-shean*
        ○ *Ibleam*

Thebez   *Jabesh-gilead?*

Pirathon   *Shechem*   *Zaphon?*

Shiloh   *Jabbok River*
                            Mizpah?

Bethel
Shaalbim *Mizpah*
Gezer ○ ○ *Aijalon*
Ekron   *Jerusalem*   Heshbon

Ashkelon

PHILISTIA

AMMON

Mediterranean Sea

Jordan River

Gaza   Hebron

Debir?

Dead Sea

Beersheba   *Arnon River*

Hormah?   **MOAB**

THEMES

The *downward spiral of unrepentant sin*, particularly *idolatry* (which means serving and worshiping a false god), is a theme that permeates the book of Judges. Nowhere in the Bible do we see more clearly what happens when people cling to idols and refuse to follow God's ways. Here we have great opportunity to learn what sin does—not only in ancient Israel but in our lives too—and to develop a hatred for it. But in the midst of sin's darkness, *the mercy and grace of God* shine through, and this is another vital theme.

Another important theme is threaded all through Judges, but it's an underlying theme, one we don't lay hold of until the end—*the need for a king*. This underlying theme is actually the most important theme in the book, and, in fact, it's the primary reason that Judges was written in the first place. If you're wondering why that matters so much—and how this theme of kingship is even relevant today—just hang on. We're going to learn why we need a king just as much as Israel did back in the dark days of the judges.

STUDYING JUDGES

At the beginning of each week's lesson, read the entire passage. And then read it again. If you are studying Judges with a group, read at least key portions of it once more, aloud, when you gather to discuss the lesson. *Marinating in the Scripture text is the most important part of any Bible study.*

GROUP STUDY

If you are doing this study as part of a group, you'll want to finish each week's lesson before the group meeting. You can work your way through the study questions all in one sitting or by doing a little bit each day. And don't be discouraged if you don't have sufficient time to answer every question. Just do as much as you can, knowing that the more you do, the more you'll learn. No matter how much of the study you are able to complete each week, the group will benefit simply from your presence, so don't skip the gathering if you can't finish! That being said, group time will be most rewarding for every participant if you have done the lesson in advance.

If you are leading the group, you can download the free leader's guide at https://www.lydiabrownback.com/flourish-series.

INDIVIDUAL STUDY

The study is designed to run for ten weeks, but you can set your own pace if you're studying solo. And you can download the free leader's guide (https://www.lydiabrownback.com/flourish-series) if you'd like some guidance along the way.

Marinating in the Scripture text is the most important part of any Bible study.

Reading Plan

	Primary Text	Supplemental Reading
Week 1	Judges 1:1–3:6	Genesis 49:8–12; Numbers 14:5–10; Deuteronomy 7:1–4; 9:5
Week 2	Judges 3:7–31	Genesis 19:30–37; Deuteronomy 23:3–4; 32:15–18; Psalm 115:4–8; Isaiah 44:9–20
Week 3	Judges 4:1–5:31	Genesis 3:15; 1 Thessalonians 5:1–10
Week 4	Judges 6:1–8:35	Exodus 33:18–20; Numbers 25:1–13; 31:1–12
Week 5	Judges 9:1–10:5	Deuteronomy 11:26–32; Joshua 8:33; 2 Samuel 23:3–7; Jeremiah 17:5–8; Luke 6:43–45
Week 6	Judges 10:6–12:15	Leviticus 5:4–6; 22:18–20; Numbers 20:14–21; 21:21–25; Deuteronomy 18:9–12
Week 7	Judges 13:1–16:31	Numbers 6:1–21; 1 Samuel 1:1–18; Luke 1:5–17
Week 8	Judges 17:1–18:31	Genesis 49:17; Exodus 20:4–6; 40:12–15; Deuteronomy 12:10–14; Psalm 7:14–16; Isaiah 1:11–17; 46:6–7; Revelation 19:11–16
Week 9	Judges 19:1–20:48	Genesis 19:1–11; Ephesians 5:25–29; 1 Peter 3:7
Week 10	Judges 21:1–25	1 Samuel 8:4–7; 2 Samuel 7:4–17; Psalm 89:19–29; Isaiah 9:6–7; Luke 1:30–33; John 19:16–22; 1 Timothy 6:13–16; Hebrews 11:32–34; Revelation 17:14

CARELESSNESS AND COMPROMISE

JUDGES 1:1-3:6

"After the death of Joshua"—the very first words of Judges tell us exactly where we are in Bible history. The leader of God's people, Joshua, has died. Who will lead them now? Joshua will be a tough act to follow. He'd lived his life in courageous obedience to God. Completing the work begun by his mentor Moses, Joshua had led Israel, God's people, out of the wilderness and into Canaan, the land God had promised to give them as their very own possession.

So here at the beginning of our story, we find Israel in Canaan, the promised land, but there's a big problem. God's people aren't living in faith and obedience. God had given them this land gift, but in order to prosper as God intended—worshiping him and enjoying an abundance of spiritual and material blessings—he'd instructed them to dislodge the wicked people already living there, distinct regions of people who together are called the "Canaanites." In fact, God had commanded Israel not simply to dislodge the Canaanites but actually to wipe out those ungodly people:

> When the Lord your God brings you into the land that you are entering to take possession of it, and clears away many nations before you, the Hittites, the Girgashites, the Amorites, the Canaanites, the Perizzites, the Hivites, and the Jebusites, seven nations more numerous and mightier than you, and when the Lord your God gives them over to you, and you defeat them,

then you must devote them to complete destruction. You shall make no covenant with them and show no mercy to them. You shall not intermarry with them, giving your daughters to their sons or taking their daughters for your sons, for they would turn away your sons from following me, to serve other gods. Then the anger of the Lord would be kindled against you, and he would destroy you quickly. (Deuteronomy 7:1–4)

At this point, perhaps you're wondering how a loving God could ever command one group of people to kill whole towns full of other people. Was Israel more righteous than the Canaanites? Did God love only Israel and hate the people of Canaan? We get our answer from what Moses had told them back before they even got to Canaan:

Not because of your righteousness or the uprightness of your heart are you going in to possess their land, but because of the wickedness of these nations the Lord your God is driving them out from before you, and that he may confirm the word that the Lord swore to your fathers, to Abraham, to Isaac, and to Jacob. (Deuteronomy 9:5)

The wickedness of the Canaanites had reached its peak, and God was ready to judge them for their sin. Israel was simply God's instrument of judgment at this particular time for these particular people. God is never doing just one thing at a time. There are always multiple layers and levels and purposes underlying his actions. So in executing judgment on the Canaanites, the Israelites were better able to safeguard their commitment to God. If they'd been given unrestricted freedom to live among people who loved evil and worshiped false gods, they'd be tempted away from the true God.

This is where we find ourselves here in Week 1. God had brought his people Israel to the promised land and given it as his gift to them. In the process of taking hold of this great gift, Israel was supposed to be God's instrument of judgment against the wicked Canaanites. But Israel had not obeyed God's command to eradicate all those bad influences. The Canaanites were still living in their midst. So Israel decides to make a fresh start of obedience.

1. ONE STEP FORWARD, TWO BACK (1:1–36)

We're introduced to a lot of people in the first chapter of Judges—so many, in fact, that we could easily bog down in the details. So we'll focus on just a few. Front and center are the twelve tribes that together make up the nation of Israel. The land of Canaan had been promised specifically to these tribes, the descendants of the twelve

The Twelve Tribes

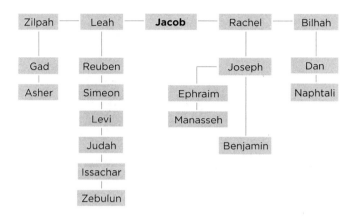

sons of Jacob the patriarch. (You can learn the backstory of Jacob and his sons in Genesis 29–30; 48–50.) The land had been divided up among them, with a couple of exceptions. First, the tribe of Levi was allotted no land. This tribe—the Levites—were the priests of God's people, so they were called to live alongside the other tribes and minister to them. The second exception is Joseph. His portion of land went directly to his two sons Ephraim and Manasseh, which elevated their status in Israel. That bit of background gives us a handle on who's who in this first chapter as the tribes rally to oust the wicked Canaanites.

✤ Israel prays for God's guidance about who should take charge (1:1). Who does God name in verse 2? How does God's answer reflect a prophecy made way back in Genesis 49:8–12, when Jacob was blessing his twelve sons—the twelve tribes—before his death?

The Allotment of the Promised Land[4]

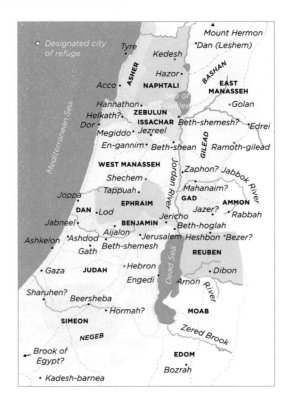

✤ In 1:3–4 we see the men from the tribe of Judah partner with the men from the tribe of Simeon, and they make some inroads in defeating their enemies. So far, so good, right? It would seem so. Until we get to the part about a local ruler named Adoni-bezek (1:5–7). Based on God's earlier instructions in Deuteronomy 7:1–2; 20:16–18, how does Israel fail to fully obey the Lord in their treatment of Adoni-bezek?

The Premier Place of Judah	
Genesis 49:8-10	Jacob blessed his sons before he died, foretelling the mighty empire that will arise through his son Judah.
Judges 1:2	The Lord chooses Judah to lead all the tribes to conquer the promised land.
Matthew 1:1-16	The ultimate savior, deliverer, and judge—Jesus Christ—comes from the line of Judah.

The tribe of Judah presses ahead with the takeover, and they have significant success, capturing a city called Jerusalem and other regions of Canaan. As the conquest of land continues, the author does a flashback in 1:10–15, weaving his story around to an earlier episode (recorded also in Joshua 15:13–19). This earlier episode involves a man named Caleb, who, long ago, had played a key role in initially leading fearful Israelites out of the wilderness and into the land of Canaan. (You can see how Caleb did that in Numbers 14:5–10.)

The flashback recorded for us here in 1:10–15 occurred after Israel had come into Canaan. What happened was that Caleb offered an incentive—marriage to his daughter Achsah—to anyone who'd step up to conquer the territory called Debir, or Kiriath-sepher. Caleb's nephew Othniel stepped up, and he won the hand of Achsah. We find this a bit shocking in our day, but back then, the arrangement would likely have dignified Achsah, and it's likely that she welcomed the opportunity to marry a military hero.

✦ Achsah may have embraced marriage to Othniel, but she didn't like the portion of land where she'd have to live with her new husband because it was "Negeb," which means it was dry and desert-like. What changed these circumstances?

✦ Judah forges ahead with the conquest in 1:16–18, accepting help from descendants of Moses's father-in-law and the tribe of Simeon. And in verse 19 we're told that, most importantly, the Lord is with Judah. What reason is given for why Judah had only partial victory?

....

....

....

....

....

They did not destroy the peoples,
    as the Lord commanded them,
but they mixed with the nations
    and learned to do as they did.
They served their idols,
    which became a snare to them.
They sacrificed their sons
    and their daughters to the demons;
they poured out innocent blood,
    the blood of their sons and daughters,
whom they sacrificed to the idols of Canaan,
    and the land was polluted with blood.
Thus they became unclean by their acts,
    and played the whore in their deeds.
(Psalm 106:34–39)

....

✛ How should we evaluate this failure in light of the promises given to Israel in Deuteronomy 20:1–4?

....

....

....

....

✛ Next to jump into battle is "the house of Joseph" (1:22), which is a way to refer to the half-tribes of Ephraim and Manasseh, Joseph's sons. In verses 22–25, how do these particular Israelites, the descendants of Joseph, fail to obey the Lord?

....

....

....

....

✛ The rest of chapter 1 (vv. 27–35) lists how all the rest of the tribes—the northern tribes—also failed to fully obey the Lord's commands concerning their takeover of Canaan. How did they fail, and what was the result?

....

....

....

....

2. SAD CONSEQUENCES (2:1–12)

Suddenly out of nowhere comes a divine messenger with a word from the Lord. Speaking on God's behalf, the messenger reminds the people of their past, recounting how God had delivered an earlier generation from slavery in Egypt and had later brought the growing nation of Israel into the promised land.

✤ According to 2:1–2, what promise had God made with that earlier generation, and what concrete acts of obedience was Israel supposed to offer in return?

✤ What consequence now awaits them in verse 3, and how do the people respond?

✤ Starting with the former leader Joshua, the narrator of our story gives one more quick overview of Israel's past in 2:6–10. What do we learn here about the spiritual condition of Israel while Joshua was living? What changed after he died?

✤ There is a vitally important connection between 2:10 and 2:11. In other words, God's people did evil (v. 11) because they did not know the Lord (v. 10). What specific evil does the narrator identify in 2:11–12?

✦ How does the Lord respond to Israel's disobedience?

....

....

....

....

3. DOWNWARD SPIRAL (2:13-23)

At the beginning of chapter 2, Israel was reminded of God's promise never to break his covenant—his relational pledge—to love, protect, and provide for them even when they sin. The Lord's unshakable commitment to care for his people is a reality we'll see all through our study. Although God gives Israel into the hands of enemies, he turns around and provides them with a way out. His purpose with his people—even in judgment—is always designed for their long-term good. Even so, a pattern is set in this section, a downward spiral, that will play out for the rest of the book.

We can trace this pattern beginning in 2:13, when Israel turns away from God to worship idols. In time, God's anger is stirred so he removes his hedge of protection from them (2:14), and they can no longer stand up against their enemies (2:15). With your Bible open to this passage, see if you can trace the pattern of this downward spiral.

2:13 *Israel turns to false gods.*

2:14 *Israel is plundered.*

2:15 *Israel is in distress.*

2:16 *The Lord raises up deliverers (judges).*

2:18 *The Lord works through the judges to deliver Israel from oppression.*

2:19 *At ease once again, Israel turns away from the Lord.*

2:20 *God brings oppression and distress on Israel.*

Can you see that Israel ended up right where they started? The full circle we see here is repeated over and over again in Judges, so much so that it's commonly called "the Judges cycle."

✦ Look more closely at 2:17. How do the people respond to God's provision of these deliverers called "judges"?

....

....

....

....

✦ According to 2:18, how and why does God work through these judges on behalf of his people?

....

....

....

....

✦ How does God use the remaining Canaanites in the lives of his people, and for what purpose (2:21–22)?

....

....

....

....

4. TIME FOR TESTING (3:1-6)

For a long time Israel has tried to get by with compromises here and there. They've half-heartedly followed God's command to possess the promised land, but they've also taken the easy way out, making peace with people God had instructed them to annihilate and settling in among them. Israel is about to learn that partial obedience is actually disobedience.

✦ How does God test, or discipline, his people here?

....

....

....

....

✦ What, in 3:5–6, does God's test expose about the people of Israel? Let Deuteronomy 7:1–6 guide your answer.

....

....

....

....

LET'S TALK

1. We are told in 2:10 that the generation of Israelites we are studying here in Judges "did not know the LORD or the work that he had done for Israel." Discuss the impact this had on the people. What does this teach us, and how can we apply it in our lives and families?

....

....

....

....

....

....

....

....

2. Before Israel even got near Canaan, the promised land, God had given clear instructions for dealing with the Canaanites who lived there (Deuteronomy 7:2–4). They were to completely remove them from the land, refusing to intermarry or to partner with them in any way. Sadly, as we end this week's lesson, we see Israel living in blatant violation of God's command, grieving God and bringing misery on themselves. This teaches us the kind of relationship God wants with his people—one of exclusive loyalty built on trust and obedience. And the Lord wants such a relationship not just with Israel, but with all his people for all time, including us. Today, rather than conquering God's enemies, we're told to love those who don't know the Lord and share with them the good news of the gospel. Even so, we live in a society that revels in worldly ways, and it's so easy to be conformed to the ungodly air we breathe in every day. Using the following passages as a guide, discuss some practical ways we can safeguard ourselves in the pursuit of holiness: Romans 12:1–2; Galatians 5:16–23; Ephesians 5:6–11, 15–21.

GOING DOWN

JUDGES 3:7-31

We encounter our first three judges this week—Othniel, Ehud, and Shamgar. But before we look at these three and what they did, we need to step back and ask, who exactly were the judges? There are twelve of them in our study, and they were obviously significant, since this book of the Bible is named for them. These twelve weren't like the judges who preside in courtrooms today. They did carry out a sort of judicial function, but primarily they were rulers with military skill who'd been raised up by God to deliver Israel from Canaanite enemies. Even though the book is named for these judges, they aren't the primary focus of our study. Our focus is the one who called and empowered each judge—the Lord God of Israel. And our takeaway isn't supposed to be anything we learn from the judges; it's the one they foreshadowed—the ultimate judge and deliverer Jesus Christ.

The Judges of Israel[5]

The Judges						
Judge	Reference	Tribe	Oppressor	Period of Oppression	Period of Rest	Total Length of Time*
Othniel	3:7-11	Judah	Mesopotamians	8 years (3:8)	40 years (3:11)	48 years
Ehud	3:12-30	Benjamin	Moabites	18 years (3:14)	80 years (3:30)	98 years
Shamgar	3:31		Philistines			
Deborah	chs. 4–5	Ephraim	Canaanites	20 years (4:3)	40 years (5:31)	60 years
Gideon	chs. 6–8	Manasseh	Midianites	7 years (6:1)	40 years (8:28)	47 years
Tola	10:1-2	Issachar			23 years (10:2)	23 years
Jair	10:3-5	Gilead-Manasseh			22 years (10:3)	22 years
Jephthah	10:6-12:7	Gilead-Manasseh	Ammonites		24 years (10:8; 12:7)	24 years
Ibzan	12:8-10	Judah or Zebulun?			7 years (12:9)	7 years
Elon	12:11-12	Zebulun			10 years (12:11)	10 years
Abdon	12:13-15	Ephraim			8 years (12:14)	8 years
Samson	chs. 13–16	Dan	Philistines	40 years (13:1)	20 years (15:20; 16:31)	60 years

*Added together, the dates in this column total about 410 years. However, many of the episodes in Judges overlap each other, unfolding in different parts of the land.

1. DOWN, DOWN, DOWN (3:7-11)

The downward spiral, the cycle we identified in 2:13–19, gives us a blueprint, a pattern, for the entire book: first sin, then enslavement, then cries for help, and finally deliverance. The pattern begins to play out here.

Trace the pattern from the following verses.

3:7 ....

3:8 ....

3:9–10 ....

3:11 ....

According to 3:7, how did worshiping the false gods—the Baals and the Asheroth—impact Israel's heart for God?

....

....

....

....

Canaanite Gods

The Canaanites believed in a creator god named El, who produced seventy children with his mistress Asherah, the goddess of fertility. One of their offspring was Baal, who became lots of lesser Baals at different times and places—something we see in the Bible with names like Baal-Peor and Baal-hermon. Over time, Baal became the primary god of Canaan because the people believed he could prevent storms, control the sea, and produce good harvests. Baal was often depicted as a bull.

The fertility goddess Asherah was portrayed as female with large breasts, and she was typically worshiped near trees, sometimes called "Asherah poles" in the Bible. Worship of Asherah involved sexual rituals. The term *Asherah* is also used for the sacred wooden poles at places where she was worshiped.

Later we'll encounter Ashtoreth, a goddess of fertility, love, and war who was linked romantically to Baal. The plural of her name, used to refer to her multiple forms, is Ashtaroth.[6]

The Canaanites believed that these false gods and goddesses, the Baals and the Ashtaroth, could bless them with fertile crops and fertile wombs. To try to get these blessings, sacrifices were made to those fertility idols, carved wooden figures with exaggerated sexual organs. And certain rituals—sexual performances—were carried out at designated worship sites.

In light of all God had done for his people over many generations, we have to wonder why Israel would be tempted to bow down to these false gods that were not God. It just makes no sense, right? After all, God was the one who'd given them this land and all its riches. So to help us understand, let's see what Scripture tells us about idols.

✦ Jot down what you learn about idols from the following passages.

· Psalm 115:4–8

....

....

....

· Isaiah 44:9–20

....

....

....

✦ Read a song written by Moses in Deuteronomy 32:15–18. Long before Israel entered into the promised land of Canaan, Moses prophesied in this song that Israel, whom he calls "Jeshurun" here, would reject God once they got there. According to Moses's prophecy, what led the people to forsake God?

....

....

....

....

✦ What else do we learn about idols from Deuteronomy 32:15–18? Look also at Psalm 106:34–39 and 1 Corinthians 10:18–20.

....

....

....

....

....

> *"To commit ourselves to some part of the creation more than to the Creator is idolatry. And when we worship something in creation, we become like it, as spiritually lifeless and insensitive to God as a piece of wood, rock, or stone."*[7]

So now that we have a bit more insight into the nature of idols, we can grasp why Israel was tempted to bow down to the Baals and the Ashtaroth. Idols have no actual substance. They aren't real. Idols are manufactured in people's hearts and are then given some sort of shape by human hands. People make idols because they want a god that they can control, one that will bless them in the way and time they want. The Lord God of the Bible doesn't bless that way. He blesses on his terms, not ours. So when answers to prayer are delayed, or when we linger in a season of suffering, we too might be tempted to set up idols to help us. And these temptations are encouraged by demons.

The Baals and Ashtaroth don't tempt us today, but we do make idols—comfort, pleasure, youth, beauty, success, romance. We might not bow down to wooden figurines, but we're tempted to worship other kinds of idols, like our bank account or our workout at the gym or our home décor. The point is, we can't really shake our heads and tsk-tsk Israel, because we carry the same idolatrous inclinations in our own hearts. We, too, so easily forsake the Lord and seek our security in something or someone else.

Idols never bless. They only take away, which is what Judges shows us. That's because God has designed us to flourish only as we worship him. When we center our hearts and lives on God through the Lord Jesus Christ, we are transformed to be more and more like Jesus. God made us in such a way that we are always conformed to what we focus on. Think about where that leads unrepentant idol worshipers. "Those who make them become like them," we're told in Psalm 115:8.

> "*What we revere, we resemble,*
> *either for ruin or restoration.*"[8]

Israel forsakes the Lord and returns to the Baals and the Asheroth, so the Lord lets them fall into the hands of a tyrant named Cushan-rishathaim. For eight long years God's people are subjected to this wicked king. Finally, in desperation, Israel cries to the Lord for help. Is Israel really ready to give up seeking help from the Baals and the Asheroth and trust in the Lord? We have to wonder, because nowhere are we told that the cries of distress included any sort of sorrow for sin or of longing to renew their relationship with God. It may be that they just want relief anywhere they think they can get it.

✦ What are we told in 3:9–10 about the deliverer God raises up, and what was the source of his power?

_____

_____

_____

_____

2. THE EDGY STORY OF EHUD (3:12–30)

The second judge, a deliverer sent by God, was a man named Ehud from the tribe of Benjamin. We're told little about Ehud other than that he was a left-handed man. Very likely, left-handedness was a desirable trait for powerful warriors because it helped them handle certain types of weapons. Ehud comes on the scene after Israel has once again turned away from the Lord to mingle with the ungodly Canaanites and worship their gods. In this section we can once again identify the downward pattern: Israel sins, so the Lord lets them taste the bitterness of their disobedience. Yet when they cry out to him for help, he raises up someone to deliver them.

✤ The oppression of Israel at this time includes heavy taxes, which they are required to pay to King Eglon of Moab. What do you learn about the Moabites from the following passages?

· Genesis 19:30–37

· Deuteronomy 23:3–4

✤ When tax day approaches, Israel sends their new deliverer, Ehud, to King Eglon with the tax money. Ehud clearly has a well-developed strategy. How does Ehud manage to get a private audience with King Eglon?

✤ When Ehud approaches the king in his chamber, he says, "I have a message from God for you" (3:20). What was that message?

How does Ehud trick the king's servants so he can make a clean getaway?

What impressions do you get of both Ehud and Eglon from how the author unfolds the story?

· Ehud:

· Eglon:

What did God bring about for his people through raising up Ehud?

3. SHAMGAR (3:31)

Shamgar is the third judge God raises up to deliver his people. We know very little about Shamgar other than that he likely was not an Israelite. If that is indeed the case, it's one example of how God uses all kinds of people—not just those within his covenant—to accomplish his purposes. Shamgar is called "the son of Anath," which indicates that he could have come from a family that worshiped Anath, a Canaanite warrior goddess. Shamgar is credited with killing six hundred Philistines with an ox-goad, a spiked stick used to prod farm animals.

✦ When we look at the last portion of 3:30, which leads into the deliverance Shamgar provides, what is missing from the usual downward cycle?

LET'S TALK

1. We aren't tempted to worship fertility statues today, but we are tempted to make other kinds of idols. Discuss what you learned about idols this week and how idols get a grip on us. What particular idols tend to draw you away from trusting in the Lord? Discuss when and why you find yourself tempted.

2. In the Old Testament we see the Spirit of God, the Holy Spirit, empowering individuals for the good of God's people. The Spirit is revealed numerous times in Judges, the first appearance being this week with Othniel (3:10). In the New Testament, after Jesus ascended back to the Father in heaven, the Spirit began to come on God's people in a deeper, richer way than ever before. Look first at the Spirit in Judges 3:10; 6:34; 11:29; 14:6, 19; 15:14, and then read John 16:7–11 and Acts 2:1–4. Keeping in mind what you see here, discuss the role of the Holy Spirit in your walk with the Lord and how his presence with you as a believer in Christ is different from what we see of his ways in Judges.

A TALE OF TWO WOMEN

JUDGES 4:1-5:31

Deborah and Jael—two notable women. Each in her own way advances God's purposes for his people. It's been said of Deborah that "this remarkable woman is without doubt the most honorable human figure in . . . Judges and one of the most remarkable characters in the entire Old Testament."⁹ Jael is a bit harder to label. We are told little about her, but what we do see is quite shocking. We can only watch in horrified fascination as she uses her wits to rid Israel of a formidable enemy. Along with these two women, this week we meet Barak the Israelite warrior. Opposing him is Sisera, the commander of the Canaanite army. As we make our way through Judges 4, we find ourselves in the midst of another episode of Israel's downward cycle. Afterward, in chapter 5, we find something unique in the book of Judges—a triumphant song of praise to the Lord, which was composed by Deborah to celebrate the Lord's faithfulness. As you budget your study time this week, it might be helpful to know that Week 3 is a tad shorter than some, while the next week, Week 4, runs longer. We have to allow for this sort of unevenness from time to time in order to stay in tune with the flow of the biblical text. So if you finish one of the shorter lessons earlier than you planned, you might want to get a head start on the following week.

1. A COMPELLING WOMAN (4:1-10)

We all know from experience that sin can seem exciting at first or appealing in some way. After all, we wouldn't be tempted to sin if it were unappealing. Even so, Judges shows us that sin is actually dull and boring in its weary sameness. We see it clearly here, when Israel falls into the same old sins and spirals down in the same old cycle.

They do evil *again*, we're told, and as a result, God turns them over to a cruel Canaanite king named Jabin who, by means of his army commander Sisera, mistreats them. God's people, Israel, are powerless to help themselves, so they do what they always do in trouble—cry out to the Lord for help.

✦ What do we learn about Deborah in 4:4–5?

....

....

....

....

Deborah oversaw civil matters among God's people, deciding—judging—the best outcome for people in disputable situations. In this sense she was indeed a judge, but she was different from the other judges of the time because, as we will soon see, she didn't personally deliver Israel from the enemy. She is the only Israelite leader in the book of Judges not specifically identified as a deliverer raised up by God.

> *"In an era of weak men, God raised a woman to serve as a lightning rod against his wrath."*[10]

Given her position in Israelite society, Deborah surely knew the ins and outs, the daily happenings, of God's people, and that life under the oppressive Canaanite King Jabin had become unbearable. So she summons an Israelite warrior named Barak.

✦ Where in 4:6 can we detect a subtle rebuke in Deborah's words to Barak?

....

....

....

....

✦ What plan has the Lord outlined for Barak, and why does Barak have nothing to fear?

✦ What impression do we get of Barak as he converses with Deborah in 4:6–9, and, according to Deborah in 4:9, how will this character assessment play out?

2. A MYSTERIOUS WOMAN (4:11–23)

Smack in the middle of the story, in verse 11, we find mention of a man named Heber. For some reason, Heber had separated from the rest of his clan, the Kenites, and set up his living quarters—his tent—some distance away. What do Heber and his tent have to do with the story? We will find out soon. In the meantime, the story resumes as Sisera and Barak prepare to face each other in battle.

✦ What role does Deborah play on the day of battle?

✦ Whom does the narrator of the story credit in 4:15 with routing the Canaanite army?

✦ Now we find out why Heber the Kenite was mentioned earlier, in verse 11. He is the husband of Jael. According to verse 17, why does Sisera flee to Jael's tent?

✦ Jael's murder of Sisera seems almost surprising when we get to it in verse 21. Why do you think it shocks us so much?

We aren't told why Jael took it upon herself to murder Sisera. After all, her husband, Heber, had a good relationship with those on Sisera's side. Jael's treachery is mysterious indeed. Perhaps the answer lies in what we *aren't* told, such as why Sisera came to Jael's tent instead of to the tent of Jael's husband. Customarily the man of the family was the one to extend hospitality to visitors. Here, though, we see that Sisera fled to Jael's tent, not Heber's, and that when he arrived, she came out to meet him and welcome him inside. The whole incident is shrouded in mystery. Whatever the reason, Deborah's prophecy about Barak has come true: "The road on which you are going will not lead to your glory, for the LORD will sell Sisera into the hand of a woman" (4:9).

✦ According to verses 23 and 24, what was the eventual outcome of this battle, and who is credited with the victory?

....

....

....

....

3. A JOYOUS DUET (5:1–23)

After the death of Sisera—a humiliating defeat for the Canaanites—Deborah composes a song praising God for the victory, and together she and Barak sing the story of how it all unfolded.

✦ What do we learn in 5:2 about those who participated in the battle?

....

....

....

....

In verses 4 and 5 Deborah is likely recalling a long-ago deliverance, the time when God brought his people out of Egypt. Afterward, they entered into a brand-new covenant with him at Mount Sinai. We aren't exactly sure what Deborah has in mind when she mentions God's marching out from Seir and from the region of Edom. The overall point here in verses 4 and 5 is that the God who has delivered his people in times past will be faithful to deliver in the present and future. This is worth singing about!

If you recall, back in Judges 3:31 Shamgar saved Israel from the invading Philistines, a people who'd come into Canaan about the same time as Israel. The Philistines were more technically advanced than Israel, so they were a formidable foe. Despite Shamgar's victory, the Philistines remained a thorn in Israel's side for a long time.

✦ Here in 5:6–7 Deborah is thinking of the danger these enemies threatened, forcing God's people to cease traveling and remain at home. What changes this dire situation?

✦ What, according to verse 8, was the underlying reason for Israel's fearful circumstance?

Those who ride on white donkeys and sit on rich carpets (5:10) are Canaanites who have treated Israel callously. They are humiliated now as Deborah calls on them to acknowledge Israel's victory at the hands of Israel's powerful God.

✦ Deborah brings ten of the twelve Israelite tribes into her song in verses 14–17. She doesn't mention Judah and Simeon. Some from the ten she does mention held back, refusing to get involved in the battle: Reuben, Dan, Asher, and Gilead. (Gilead was part of the Manasseh tribe.) What do their excuses seem to indicate about their heart priorities?

Deborah's exuberance soars as she recounts in verses 20 and 21 how God works his will, giving his people military victory through even the natural world he created. Day and night and even storms are controlled by God for his glory and good purposes. In verse 23 Deborah calls a curse down on the region of Meroz because those who live there refused to join the Lord's cause and aid Israel in the battle.

> *"It speaks ill of us when we are satisfied to rest secure while our brothers and sisters are struggling and suffering."*[11]

4. WOMEN AND WAR (5:24-31)

Men go off to war while their women wait anxiously at home for news from the battle-front. Down through history, that's typically how it has played out. But that's not so in this case, where the woman Jael plays a key role in the warfare.

✦ Deborah's song recounts in detail what Jael did to Sisera. As you consider the big picture of the story so far—God's purposes for his people in the land of Canaan—why do you think Jael is celebrated as the "most blessed of women" (v. 24)?

✦ Read Genesis 3:15, where the Lord tells the serpent (Satan) that the woman's offspring will eventually crush his head. This promised defeat of the serpent is actually the very first announcement of the gospel in the Bible. Evil won't triumph! How does the episode recorded in 5:26–27 carry forward the promise of Genesis 3:15?

We can't help but feel sympathy for Sisera's mother as she watches anxiously for the return of her son. Her maidservants try to reassure her that all is well. After all, they say, it takes time to divvy up the enemy loot and, as was typical back then, the captured women. But however sorry we might feel for Sisera's mom, we have to remember that she was a Canaanite—she stood against God's people and therefore against God himself.

✦ The song ends in 5:31 with a prayerful petition. Deborah couldn't have known the full extent of God's answer to this petition. How does 1 Thessalonians 5:1–10 reveal it to us?

....

....

....

....

LET'S TALK

1. Deborah is a picture of godly womanhood, but not a typical picture. What is revealed about Deborah that leads to her godly reputation? As you consider the glimpses we're given of Deborah's character, what do you think made her so useful in the Lord's service? Discuss how she is different from what we often expect a godly woman to be like.

....

....

....

....

....

....

....

2. An entire chapter of Judges is devoted to Deborah's song of praise, which she sang with Barak after the Canaanite defeat. Years before this happened, after the Lord miraculously parted the waters of the Red Sea to deliver Israel from the Egyptians, Moses's sister Miriam sang a similar song before a group of women. "Sing to the LORD, for he has triumphed gloriously," sang Miriam, shaking her tambourine (Exodus 15:21). Both women publicly upheld the Lord as their great deliverer. How do we do with public praise, especially when it comes to victories over our own greatest enemy—sin? Are we willing to share our sin struggles with others (not necessarily an entire group, but even a friend or two) as well as the victories we enjoy through the Lord's help? Discuss how bringing others into both the struggles and the victories can glorify God and strengthen our brothers and sisters in Christ. And then, if time permits, begin right now in your group discussion!

WEAK PEOPLE, STRONG GOD

JUDGES 6:1-8:35

Forty years of peace—an entire generation of Israel enjoys the blessings of life in the promised land. But during these decades, God's people once again are careless toward the Lord, and they turn away from him and begin to worship other things—wealth and worldliness and Canaanite gods. So once again, the Lord lifts his protection so that his people experience misery and see yet again where life apart from him inevitably leads. In time, though, God raises up a new judge, Gideon, and it's his story that we're studying this week. Here we get to see glimpses of God's power and patience, yet the lesson drives home the fact that God requires exclusive loyalty from his people. We're also going to see that God loves to use weak people to accomplish his purposes.

1. "THUS SAYS THE LORD . . ." (6:1–10)

The invading enemies are like swarms of locusts. The thieving Midianites watch and wait for Israel's crops to ripen, and then they swoop in to steal the harvest, bankrupting God's people of income and food supplies. And the Midianites don't do it just once. They invade again and again for seven years so that Israel has to hide in caves just to survive. This isn't the first time that Midian has troubled God's people. Tension between Israel and Midian began way back before Israel had even come into the promised land.

✦ What does God do when Israel cries out to him for help? Why were God's people likely disappointed with this answer to their cry?

....

....

....

....

....

....

....

....

....

The Midianites

The Midianites were wanderers, and they traveled around the deserts on the fringes of Canaan. They were associated with the Ishmaelites, Amalekites, and Moabites. Long ago the Midianites had seduced Israel into worshiping a false god, Baal, and afterward they were considered Israel's enemies (see Numbers 25:1–13; 31:1–12).

✦ Through the mouth of the prophet, the Lord reminds his people of the past in 6:8–10. Who and what is the focus of this look backward?

· In verse 8:

....

....

....

· In verse 9:

....

....

....

· In verse 10:

✦ Why do you think the Lord gives this history lesson here, in the midst of such a devastating ordeal?

2. THE ANGEL OF THE LORD AND A MAN NAMED GIDEON (6:11-32)

We get to listen in here to an important conversation between the angel of the Lord and a man named Gideon. Gideon is one of the Abiezrites, a clan of Manasseh.

✦ The angel identifies Gideon as a "mighty man of valor" in 6:12. How in 6:13–18 does Gideon seem to fall short of the angel's description?

✦ How does 6:13 show that Gideon has a skewed perspective on Israel's current circumstances?

✦ The Lord is raising up Gideon to deliver Israel from the Midianites. In 6:15–16, how does Gideon try to get out of this call on his life, and how does God refute Gideon's argument?

....

....

....

....

....

....

....

Second-guessing everything at this point, Gideon asks the angel of the Lord for a sign that his call to deliver is really coming from the Lord. His desire is granted when the angel miraculously consumes Gideon's meal in flames and then suddenly vanishes.

The Angel of the Lord

The Hebrew word for "angel" can also be translated as "messenger." There is an element of mystery about this figure. When the angel of the Lord speaks, his words are perceived as God's words, so we get the impression that the angel is identical to God. It's also why some believe that "the angel of the Lord" is Jesus Christ appearing on earth before he was actually born as a man. On the other hand, he might simply be an angel sent to speak as God's representative such that the angel's words are God's words.[12]

✦ Gideon is now convinced that he's had a face-to-face divine encounter, but from what the Lord says to him in 6:23, it seems he is also afraid. In order to understand his fear, we have to look back to a similar event in Israel's history—God's call on Moses. How does the Lord's encounter with Moses in Exodus 33:18–20 explain why Gideon is afraid?

....

....

....

....

On a related note, if you've got some extra time this week, you might want to read the full story back in Exodus 33:1–23 of how God called Moses. If you do, be sure to jot down all the similarities you see between Moses's call and Gideon's. This sort of connection in the Bible is no coincidence!

✦ Gideon's first task as the new deliverer is to rip down the place where the false gods are worshiped. What is revealed about Gideon in 6:27?

....

....

....

....

....

....

....

> **Appearances of the Angel of the Lord in Judges**
>
> - to all Israel (2:1-4)
> - in Deborah's song (5:23)
> - to Gideon (6:11-12, 20-22)
> - to Samson's parents (13:3-23)

Gideon tears down the altars of the false gods, greatly angering the townspeople. Afterward Gideon's father defends his son and tries to reason with the angry mob, pointing out that a real god could take care of himself. His point was taken, so the people's anger turned to admiration, and Gideon was given a new name—Jerubbaal, which means "Let Baal contend against him."

3. GIDEON'S FAMOUS FLEECE (6:33-40)

Gideon wants reassurance. Has God really called him? After all, Midian is a powerful enemy. So he asks God for proof, a sign that God will be with him as he heads into battle. Gideon's request involves an animal fleece and some strategic placing of morning dew. When Christians are faced with a tough decision and want to know God's will, they sometimes talk about "putting out a fleece." In such cases they are trying to adapt what Gideon does here—request a sign—to their own circumstances. But it's important that we recognize that Gideon isn't asking God what he should do; rather, he is asking for confirmation about what God has *already* told him to do (you can see this clearly in 6:36–37).

✦ Two separate times Gideon asks God to perform the sign, and he includes a special plea the second time he asks. What does this seem to indicate about Gideon?

✦ Both times God gives Gideon what he asks for. What does this tell us about the Lord?

4. TO GOD BE THE GLORY (7:1-18)

Gideon has been reassured and prepares for battle. God has indeed called him to take on the Midianites, and Gideon has no need to be afraid because God will be with him every step of the way. But as soon as Gideon goes forth, his battle plan is derailed by the Lord himself.

✦ How does God thin out the army in 7:2–3, and what reason does he give for doing so?

The Lord further reduces Gideon's troops until there are only three hundred men remaining from the initial thirty-two thousand—hardly an intimidating army! Scholars have suggested all kinds of things to make sense of God's water-drinking test in 7:4–7, but we simply don't know why God chose to thin the army in this way. Ultimately, it doesn't matter because it's not the point of the story, as we shall see.

✦ The time has come. "Arise," says the Lord to Gideon, "go down against the camp, for I have given it into your hand" (7:9). Despite the Lord's reassurance, what do verses 10–11 reveal about Gideon?

✦ How in 7:13–14 does the Lord once again reassure his appointed deliverer, and how does Gideon respond?

How would you summarize the Lord's dealings with Gideon in this section, and how has Gideon changed from the beginning of the section (7:1) to the end (7:17–18)?

5. NO MORE MIGHTY MIDIAN (7:19–25)

It's midnight. Gideon and his army of three hundred creep toward Midian's camp, but their weapons are hardly intimidating—just torches and trumpets. The life-threatening swords are found only in the hands of the Midianites, but the Midianite men are so confused by Gideon's middle-of-the-night, glaringly bright, loud intrusion into their camp that they wind up turning their swords on themselves. One Bible commentator says, "This is psychological warfare at its best."[13]

What began as a large army of thirty-two thousand men had been reduced by the Lord to just three hundred, and then this small army is sent into battle with no real weapons. All along the way, the Lord reassures Gideon of victory. What does this reveal about God and how he works in the lives of his people?

The Midianites are on the lam, so Gideon calls on other Israelites—men from Ephraim— to come help the army get the job done. And this does the trick. With the execution of two Midianite princes, the war is over.

6. TROUBLE ON THE HOME FRONT (8:1–21)

Have you ever noticed how adrenaline focuses our entire being on resolving whatever threat has triggered it? Our senses are heightened, our energies are focused, and we feel this almost supernatural ability to problem solve. It seems this is what happened to the men of Ephraim, those who answered Gideon's call to roust the Midianites. But afterward, when the adrenaline was no longer flowing, the men of Ephraim reflected on how it had all come about, and as they pondered, they began to resent Gideon because he'd waited until the last minute to invite them to participate in the fight (8:1).

✦ How does Gideon calm down the angry Ephraimites in 8:2–3?

....

....

....

....

Tired and hungry, Gideon asks the men of Succoth for bread, but his request is denied. The men of Succoth realize that if Gideon were to lose to Midian, they would remain exposed and vulnerable to further Midianite attacks, and they don't want to provoke more potential problems. The same fear governs the people of Penuel, who also refuse Gideon's request.

✦ How does Gideon respond to the men of Succoth and Penuel when his request is refused?

....

....

....

....

✦ What reason does Gideon give for killing the two Midianite kings, Zebah and Zalmunna?

....

....

....

....

✦ As you ponder this section—from the time Gideon and his small army cross the Jordan River (8:1) to the slaying of the Midianite kings (8:21)—how is this venture different from Gideon's earlier battle? In other words, what seems to be missing? And related, how is Gideon himself different?

....

....

....

....

7. GIDEON'S END (8:22-35)

God's people are so relieved to be out from under the oppressive Midianites that they want their God-appointed deliverer, Gideon, to be their king. Gideon refuses, reminding them that they already have a king—the Lord God of Israel. But soon after, Gideon makes choices that contradict his refusal, one of which is taking the spoils of war to make a golden garment, a sleeveless tunic called an ephod. There's a problem though: only one ephod was allowed in Israel—the one worn by the high priest—and tucked into this ephod were tools (the Urim and Thummim) used to seek out and discover God's will in various situations. So for Gideon to make an additional ephod and set it up for his own use was just plain wrong. We aren't told why Gideon wanted access to an ephod of his own. Most likely he wanted it because he saw it as a way to guarantee getting more of God's guidance in the future and all the personal success that seemed to come with it.

✦ What happened with Gideon's ephod, and who was affected by it?

....

....

....

....

✦ After Gideon dies, the people of Israel fall into the same old sin—setting up false gods and worshiping them. In the process, what two vital things do they fail to do?

Ephod

The ephod, a sleeveless tunic placed over other clothes, was worn by the high priest. It was made from gold and expensive fabrics. Attached to the ephod was a breastplate containing twelve precious stones, one for each tribe of Israel. Inside the breastplate was a pocket for the Urim and Thummim which were used to discover God's will for various situations.

Once again God had raised up a deliverer—in this case, Gideon—to rescue his people, and once again peace was restored to the land, and Israel had rest for forty years (8:28). However, this is the last time. The cycle we've seen repeated—sin, cries for help, deliverance, rest—is coming to an end.

> *"People who by persisting apostasy despise Yahweh's gift will find that gift withdrawn."*[14]

LET'S TALK

1. Lots of people view the episode of Gideon and the fleece as something believers today can apply to their own lives when they want to know God's will for a particular decision or choice. When we hear Christians talk about "putting out a fleece," this is the story they have in mind. But as we noted, Gideon already knew God's will. The fleece was merely God's

kind way of confirming it. So if not by fleeces, how can we know God's will? Discuss how the Bible, prayer, and godly counsel factor in. You might want to take a look at Romans 12:1–2; Colossians 1:9–10; 1 Thessalonians 4:3; 5:18; Hebrews 13:20–21; and 1 Peter 4:1–3.

2. Gideon apparently served to anchor Israel's focus on the Lord, because as soon as Gideon died, the people turned back to the Baals and forgot God—not facts about God but their affection for God. In other words, they did not "remember" the Lord (8:34). Their zeal for God was external and superficial. So let's examine our own hearts: Is something or someone outside of us serving as our spiritual anchor? Or do we truly love God and desire to follow and serve him from the depths of our heart? How can we avoid allowing God's good gifts and spiritual blessings to take the place of God himself?

A VERY BAD MAN (AND TWO LITTLE-KNOWN JUDGES)

JUDGES 9:1-10:5

Gideon has died, but his legacy lives on in his seventy sons, which he fathered through his many wives. From his concubine he had another son named Abimelech. A concubine was like a second-tier wife. Gideon's concubine came from Shechem, and she was a Canaanite, so their union was a clear violation of God's instruction that his people must not enter into any sort of marriage relationship with a Canaanite (see Deuteronomy 7:3–4). This outline of Gideon's family is found back in Judges 8:29–32, which we covered last week, but it's important to bring into this week's study because the son of Gideon's concubine, Abimelech, is about to come front and center. So that will be our focus this week, and after the cringey story of Abimelech, we'll look at just a few basic facts about two judges, Tola and Jair.

1. ABIMELECH'S EVIL PLOT (9:1-6)

Abimelech chooses to align himself with the maternal side of his family—the Canaanite side—but it seems his choice has little to do with any sort of family feeling. Abimelech has an agenda.

✦ How does Abimelech manipulate his family and the other people of Shechem, and what does he hope to gain?

....

....

....

....

✦ What else do you see in this section that reveals the true character of Abimelech?

_____

_____

_____

_____

2. JOTHAM'S FABLE (9:7–21)

Abimelech is anointed king by his Shechem relatives, but what sort of king will he actually be? He not only manipulated his way to power; he murdered his own brothers to get it. Abimelech is not the sort of leader God's people—or any people—can generally profit under. When tyrannical leaders come to power, people need courage—lots of it—to speak boldly for what's right. In this case, it comes through Abimelech's only surviving brother, Jotham, who'd escaped Abimelech's treachery because he hid during the slaughter. Jotham comes out of hiding to try to shake the people of Shechem back to reality, to open their manipulated eyes to see the reality of Abimelech's character, and he does so by telling them a fable.

✦ Jotham delivers his fable from the top of Mount Gerizim. This is significant because, in Moses's day, this particular mountain had been identified as the place where God's people would be blessed once they'd entered the promised land of Canaan (Deuteronomy 11:26–32). Later, when Joshua led Israel into this land, he did what Moses had instructed and blessed the people on that mountain (Joshua 8:33). With that backstory in mind, why is this location significant for the telling of Jotham's fable?

_____

_____

_____

_____

✦ When the olive tree, the fig tree, and the vine are invited to rule, they decline. What commonality do you see in the reason each gives for saying no?

_____

_____

_____

✦ The fourth tree in the fable, the bramble, is a not so subtle jab at Abimelech. This is not the only time in Scripture that trees are used to teach an important lesson, and from some of those other instances, what can we infer about Abimelech's character?

· 2 Samuel 23:3–7

_____

· Jeremiah 17:5–8

_____

· Luke 6:43–45

_____

✦ Jot down anything from these passages that strikes you personally.

_____

Jotham's fable ends with an "if . . . then" challenge to the people of Shechem: "*If you . . . have acted in good faith and integrity with Jerubbaal [Gideon] and with his house this day, then* rejoice in Abimelech, and let him also rejoice in you" (9:19). The answer is already clear—Shechem has not acted in good faith, so ultimately there will be no rejoicing.

3. EVIL BURNS UP EVIL (9:22-57)

God has designed things in such a way that evil breeds the seeds of its own destruction. We see that clearly here. The people of Shechem are having second thoughts about Abimelech, this man they've made king. Added to that, out of nowhere comes a troublemaker named Gaal, and he succeeds in turning the people of Shechem fully against Abimelech. But Shechem's ruler Zebul remains loyal to Abimelech, and together Zebul and Abimelech plot to destroy Gaal and the other rebels.

> *"Here lies a firm comfort for God's beleaguered people: God destroys the destroyers of his people."*[15]

✦ What, according to 9:23, is the underlying cause of strife between Abimelech and the leaders of Shechem?

When Abimelech's gang closes in to attack, both Gaal and Zebul, who are standing at the entrance gate of the city, can see the them approaching. Zebul is able to convince Gaal that his eyes are playing tricks, so Gaal does nothing to protect himself until the gang is almost on top of them. As a result, Abimelech is able to drive out Gaal. Then he destroys everyone in Shechem before moving on to the nearby town of Thebez. He is on a roll and wants to conquer and destroy as much as he can.

Review God's words to the serpent in Genesis 3:15:

> I will put enmity between you and the woman,
>   and between your offspring and her offspring;
> he shall bruise your head,
>   and you shall bruise his heel.

✦ Where do we see a partial fulfillment of this curse in the way Abimelech dies, and what does this tell us about Abimelech?

....

....

....

....

✦ We learn something about how God judges unrepentant sin in 9:56–57. What do these verses show us about God's judgment?

....

....

....

....

4. TOLA AND JAIR (10:1–5)

Little is known about the next two judges, Tola and Jair, but this doesn't mean that they were insignificant. After all, God is the one who raised them up, and he surely accomplished his purposes through them, even though we do not know the specifics.

✦ What details about Tola and Jair does the author highlight for us, and which ones advance the storyline of the book?

· Tola:

....

....

....

· Jair:

....

....

....

LET'S TALK

1. We watched in horror this week as Abimelech slaughtered his brothers and manipulated his Shechem relatives in a play for power. But his evil came back on his own head—literally! What we learn from the story is that evil is often consumed by the same kind of evil. It's a pattern we see all through Scripture. Take a look at Psalm 7:14–16; Ezekiel 11:21; Obadiah 15; Galatians 6:6–7; and Revelation 17:15–17 for a sampling. As we realize that God has hardwired this sort of judgment into the ways of the world, discuss how we can be both warned and comforted. Which of the two—warning or comfort—most grabs hold of your heart and why?

....

....

....

....

....

....

....

2. Like Sisera before him (Judges 2), Abimelech died from a blow to the head administered by a woman. In both cases, we see reflections of God's words to the serpent in Genesis 3:15. Discuss how these glimpses of the promise, which was fulfilled on the cross by Jesus when he died for sin and dealt a fatal blow to the serpent, can help us when we struggle with

sin—both our own sin and the effects of others' sin. You might want to bring Hebrews 2:14–15 into your discussion.

FROM BAD TO WORSE

JUDGES 10:6-12:15

Sandwiched between some little-known judges is a better-known judge named Jephthah. The writer of our story devotes a lot of space to the circumstances of this particular judge. He rose from what today we would call an underprivileged background to serve as a warrior-leader and to deliver Israel from yet another formidable enemy. We can't help but notice, however, that something vital is missing in the story of Jephthah—the presence of the Lord. But it's not that God is absent; it's that his people aren't paying him any attention. They have forgotten him again and fallen even farther away. The consequences of abandoning God begin to show up not only nationally but also personally.

1. FROM BAD TO WORSE (10:6-16)

Same sin, different day. Can you identify the cycle? Israel does evil, and the Lord raises up an enemy—in this case, two—to get his people's attention. There's a one-two punch aimed at Israel this time, with both the Ammonites and the Philistines coming at them at once. This week's study addresses the Ammonite problem in particular.

✦ How has Israel's worship of false gods expanded over time?

As usual, when life becomes unbearable, Israel cries out to the Lord for help. What's different about their cry this time around? You might want to compare 10:10 with their earlier cries in 3:9, 15; 4:3; and 6:6.

How does the Lord's response in 10:11–14 show us the true state of his people's hearts toward him?

Consider how Israel responds to the Lord's sharp rebuke.

· What is noticeably absent in their response?

· What is their priority?

This section ends with God's impatience over Israel's misery. We can interpret this impatience in one of two ways. Either the Lord, in his mercy, is impatient to deliver his people from their sin-inflicted suffering, or he is finally fed up with their fake repentance. Based on what we know about the character of God, either or both could be true.

2. ILLEGITIMATE (10:17–11:11)

As the Ammonites infiltrate the region of Gilead, the leaders of Gilead determine that something must be done. After eighteen years, enough is enough. So they put their heads together and try to come up with a name, someone who can lead them into battle against this oppressive enemy. Eventually they select a man named Jephthah.

✦ Describe Jephthah's upbringing and where this lands him as a young man.

✦ Why is Jephthah understandably suspicious of the Gilead leaders' offer?

✦ Summarize in the space below how each judge came into the role of deliverer. What makes Jephthah's rise to the position different from the others?

· Othniel (3:7–9)

· Deborah with Barak (4:4–9)

....

....

....

· Gideon (6:11–14)

....

....

....

· Jephthah (11:4–8)

....

....

....

3. JEPHTHAH'S APPEAL (11:12-28)

Before launching headlong into war, Jephthah tries diplomacy. The Ammonites accuse Israel of stealing their land, but Jephthah, in a strongly worded speech, recounts what had *really* happened. For one thing, the Ammonites are laying claim to land that was never theirs in the first place. It had belonged to the Amorites, and long ago God had led Israel to take it over. (You might want to review that long-ago story in Numbers 21:21–25 along with the other story Jephthah recalls here concerning Moab, in Numbers 20:14–21.) So, Jephthah says, the bottom line is that the Ammonites are rewriting history, and they need to be content with the land supposedly allotted to them by the god Chemosh. Did Jephthah really believe in the existence of Chemosh or any other Canaanite god? We don't know. Perhaps this was his way of subtly mocking this false deity, getting in a good jab here, but given the state of Israel at this time—all the foreign gods they worshiped—it could very well be that Jephthah's remark reflects what he really believed at that time.

✦ What effect does Jephthah's speech have on the Ammonites?

4. A VILE VOW (11:29-40)

Jephthah prepares for war, and the Spirit of God empowers him for the battle. As he approaches the front line, Jephthah makes a vow to the Lord in hopes that the battle will go his way (11:30–31).

✦ What does Jephthah offer in his vow?

Jephthah returns from battle in triumph. The Ammonite threat has been eliminated! But as Jephthah approaches his home, he receives an emotional blow worse than any physical blow he could have experienced on the battlefield. His daughter—his only child—comes out to greet him. His vow! His terrible, awful, horrible vow! If he is to keep his vow, it seems that Jephthah must sacrifice the life of his girl.

✦ In those days it was standard practice to make vows to the Lord and to fulfill them by means of a burnt offering, but the offering was supposed to be done in the manner prescribed by the Lord himself. According to the requirements for burnt offerings found in Leviticus 22:17–20, where did Jephthah go wrong?

✦ Who in 11:35 does Jephthah blame for this awful mess?

✦ He claims he cannot take back his vow, and indeed, making a vow to the Lord is a very serious undertaking as we learn from passages such as Deuteronomy 23:21–23 and Ecclesiastes 5:4–5. At the same time, Jephthah has a way out. According to Leviticus 5:4–6, how could Jephthah be released from his vow?

✦ As you consider the responses of Jephthah and his daughter to this predicament, what contrasts can you note between the two?

Resigned to her fate, Jephthah's daughter requests time alone with her friends to mourn what will happen to her. She asks for two months to weep for her virginity (11:37), to lament that she will never have the chance to be intimate with a man in marriage. Because of this request, some think that Jephthah's vow was about committing his daughter to lifelong virginity as a symbolic sacrifice to the Lord.[16] But very likely, the awful reality is that he put her to death, sacrificing her life as a burnt offering.

✦ As we consider the very likely possibility that Jephthah sacrificed his daughter's life, how does Deuteronomy 18:9–12 shed light on the spiritual condition of Israel at this point?

5. THE ARROGANCE OF EPHRAIM (12:1-7)

"Why?" Ephraim's question in 12:1 is really a complaint. And this isn't the first time (take a look back at 8:1–3). The people of Ephraim feel slighted again, cut out of the victory over the Ammonites. It seems they are selfishly concerned only about their own tribe rather than about Israel as a whole.

✦ Why, according to Jephthah's response, does Ephraim have no right to feel slighted?

As a result, a battle is waged—Israelite against Israelite—and the men of Ephraim fall to Gilead by the simple mispronunciation of a word. Comical as that might seem, God's people have gone from battling Canaanites to battling each other. Lower and lower they go.

6. IBZAN, ELON, AND ABDON (12:8-15)

The narrator of our story tucks in a bit about three more judges: Ibzan, Elon, and Abdon.

✦ Of the little bit of information we're given, what does the narrator choose to tell us about each of these judges?

· Ibzan:

· Elon:

....

....

....

· Adbon:

....

....

....

LET'S TALK

1. Jephthah was a weak father who failed his daughter, which, sadly, some of us can relate to. Even so, every father—even the best kind—is a sinner and therefore sure to make parenting mistakes. Discuss how both terrible fathers and terrific fathers point us to our heavenly Father and help us relate to him as daughters. Consider Deuteronomy 8:5; Matthew 7:11; Hebrews 12:7–10; James 1:17; and any other passages that come to mind.

....

....

....

....

....

....

....

2. Jephthah made a vow to the Lord, one he should—and could—have broken when he realized the implications. Scripture shows us that vows are serious business, especially vows made before the Lord. We make vows when we stand at the altar to get married and when we commit to telling the truth in a court of law. Apart from these, we all regularly commit to keep our word in a variety of contexts. Discuss the following:

· When is keeping your word most challenging?

· Are you keeping a longtime vow but wondering if you are free to break it at this point? How can you find guidance?

· Identify the sort of situation in which it is better to break your word than to keep it.

PHYSICALLY STRONG BUT MORALLY WEAK

JUDGES 13:1–16:31

Strong. That's the best way to describe the twelfth and final judge in our story. Samson was physically strong, and he was also strong-willed. But Samson had great weaknesses too. Undisciplined sexual desires, romantic entanglements, and personal pride led to his downfall. Even so, God planned long before Samson's birth that he would use this flawed man in powerful ways to deliver his people. Leading into all this is the same old problem. God's people have turned away from him, so God has allowed them to be oppressed by the ungodly people still living in Canaan. This week the enemy we encounter is the Philistines—a well-entrenched and formidable foe. The cycle repeats, but this time there's something different—the people don't cry out to the Lord for deliverance. What amazing grace this is, that God comes to rescue his people anyway!

1. MIRACLE BABY (13:1–25)

A childless couple, a man named Manoah and his wife, lived in a town called Zorah, which was situated in land that belonged to the tribe of Dan.

✣ When the angel of the Lord appears to Manoah's wife and tells her she is going to have a baby, what two things does he tell her about this child in 13:4–5?

1. ....

2. ....

✦ Manoah is the one who prays in 13:8 that the angel will return and give them more information about this child, but to whom does the angel first direct his answer?

....

....

....

....

Samson is to be set apart as a Nazirite for his entire life. Becoming a Nazirite meant taking a vow to abstain from drinking alcohol, from shaving body hair, and from touching a dead body. The practice was set in place by the Lord himself back in the days of Moses, and you can read the details in Numbers 6:1–21. The vow was usually made by someone for a limited time, and afterward the Nazirite would return to normal living. Today we do something similar when we set aside time to fast and pray. For Samson, however, the vow was to be lifelong, beginning even in his mother's womb, which is why his mother was forbidden to drink wine.

✦ Two other men in the Bible, the prophets Samuel and John the Baptist, came into the world in similar circumstances. Note the similarities and differences in the chart below.

	Samson (Judges 13:2–14)	Samuel (1 Samuel 1:1–18)	John the Baptist (Luke 1:5–17)
The role of the mother			
The role of the father			

	Samson (Judges 13:2-14)	Samuel (1 Samuel 1:1-18)	John the Baptist (Luke 1:5-17)
The birth announcement			
The Nazirite vow			

Here we get a big look at how the Bible is actually tied together into one big story. These three unique men—Samson, Samuel, and John—are tied together by one overarching detail: their calling in life was to prepare the way for a king in Israel. Samson and Samuel prepared the way for King David, and John the Baptist prepared the way for David's descendant, the be-all-end-all king, King Jesus.

✦ Manoah tries to get more from the angel—a meal, even just his name—but the angel just directs Manoah to worship the Lord, and then he departs. When Manoah realizes the angel's identity, he is afraid and laments to his wife, "We shall surely die, for we have seen God" (13:22). How does Exodus 33:18–20 explain why Manoah thought they might lose their lives?

....

....

....

....

✦ How does Manoah's wife speak wisdom into her husband's fear in verse 23?

Stories of Some Barren Women in Scripture
Sarah (Genesis 16:1–6; 17:1–21; 18:1–15; 21:1–7)   Rebekah (Genesis 25:19–26)   Rachel (Genesis 29:31–30:24)   Hannah (1 Samuel 1)   Elizabeth (Luke 1)

✦ How does the Spirit of the Lord come into the story at the end of this section?

2. SAMSON GETS MARRIED (14:1–20)

Here begins the first twenty years of Samson's adult life. (The story of his adulthood is broken down for us into two parts of twenty years each.) Samson decides to visit the town of Timnah, which was occupied by the Philistine people.

✦ Why do Samson's parents object to Samson's would-be bride?

✤ What reason does Samson give for insisting on marrying her, and what does this tell us about Samson?

✤ What do we learn in 14:4 about the Lord's involvement in Samson's attraction to the Philistine woman?

✤ What enables Samson to conquer the ferocious lion?

✤ How does Samson break his Nazirite vow when he takes the honey from the lion's carcass? (You might want to take another look at Numbers 6:1–21 to review the details of the Nazirite vow.)

Not only does Samson break his vow; he defiles his parents too when he gives them honey to eat, because the location of the honeycomb—inside an animal carcass—violated God's law: "All that walk on their paws, among the animals that go on all fours, are unclean to you. Whoever touches their carcass shall be unclean until the evening" (Leviticus 11:27).

Afterward, down in Timnah, Samson gets ready for a big bachelor party. From the Hebrew word for "feast" that the narrator uses, we know that Samson's party was centered on alcohol, and if he partook, which, given his self-indulgent character, we have no reason to doubt, it was another violation of his Nazirite vow. As the party kicks off, the Philistines of Timnah bring thirty men to join the fun. Very likely, they were sent in order to keep an eye on this Israelite Samson.

During the party Samson decides to have a bit of fun with these men by posing a riddle. If they can solve it, he will give all thirty of them new clothes. If not, the men will have to supply Samson with a new wardrobe. Of course the riddle, which had to do with the honey inside the dead lion, is virtually unsolvable by anyone but Samson. Eventually the partygoers get frustrated, and they threaten Samson's wife so that she'll do whatever it takes to get the answer out of her husband.

✦ How does Samson's wife learn the secret of the riddle?

✦ Samson is very angry, but he keeps his word, acquiring clothes to give to the winners of the bet, the ones who could answer the riddle. Where and how does the Spirit of the Lord appear in this segment?

3. A BATTERED WIFE (15:1-8)

Despite all that's happened, Samson apparently believes life can simply go on as normal. No longer angry, he wants some intimacy with his wife, but his father-in-law stops him.

✦ What has happened to Samson's wife at this point, and how does her father try to appease Samson?

Clearly humiliated and even angrier than before—and showing no regard for anyone or anything—Samson gets revenge by burning down the Philistines' grain harvest and olive produce.

✦ What is the outcome for Samson's wife?

4. FIGHTING THE PHILISTINES (15:9-20)

It's all-out war at this point. The Philistines are fed up with Samson, and they make a raid on Lehi in the territory of Judah.

✦ The men of Judah want nothing to do with the fight between Samson and the Philistines. What do the men of Judah say in 15:11 that lets us know they are no longer even trying to follow the Lord's command to rid the land of pagan enemies?

✦ Why do you think the men of Judah don't just go ahead and kill Samson themselves?

....

....

....

....

✦ How does the Spirit of the Lord come into the story in 15:14–15?

....

....

....

....

The fact that Samson's weapon, a jawbone, had come from a recently deceased animal is key to understanding what happened here. An old jawbone would have been dry and brittle, easily broken. This fresh one stayed intact as it delivered countless blows. Even so, utilizing the jawbone, which came from a corpse, was yet another violation of his Nazirite vow.

✦ Following his great victory over the Philistines, what complaint does Samson make to the Lord, and how does the Lord respond?

....

....

....

....

In 15:20 the narrator tells us that Samson "judged Israel in the days of the Philistines twenty years." This indicates to us that he's wrapping up the first half of Samson's story. Later on, the narrator will end the second half in a similar way (16:31).

5. SAMSON'S NIGHT IN GAZA (16:1-3)

Samson was the rare Israelite who had little fear of entering Philistine towns and doing whatever he pleased. That's why, when Samson is walking around the town of Gaza and a prostitute catches his eye, he has no qualms about enjoying her sexual favors. The men of Gaza use this opportunity, when Samson is preoccupied with lust, to plan a surprise attack on him. When night comes, they lie in wait for him at the city gate. But Samson catches on, foils their plot, and humiliates his would-be attackers by uprooting the city's heavy iron gate and walking off with it unharmed.

✦ Based on what we know about the source of Samson's strength, how was he able to escape the ambush and walk safely out of Gaza?

6. SAMSON AND DELILAH (16:4-31)

As he wanders down in the Valley of Sorek, Samson falls head over heels for a woman named Delilah. Never one to practice discernment in romantic entanglements, Samson's relationship with Delilah is no exception. In fact, it proves to be his downfall.

✦ By what means is Delilah encouraged to trap Samson, and what incentive is she offered to do so?

✦ Samson sees right through her manipulative tactics and teases her. He seems undisturbed by her not so subtle attempts to bring him harm. Why do you think he overlooks or fails to see what she is doing?

_____

_____

_____

_____

✦ How does Delilah finally get Samson to reveal the secret of his strength?

_____

_____

_____

_____

Once Samson reveals his secret, his supernatural strength vanishes because the Lord leaves him. His strength was never in his hair but in the Lord, who empowered him as he lived out—however imperfectly—his life as a Nazirite. In reality, Samson departed from the Lord before the Lord left him. But it's important to clarify that what "left" Samson was the Lord's empowering, not his presence or his providential care.

✦ The narrator tells us in 16:22 that Samson's hair begins to grow again. What do you think is the spiritual significance of the regrowth?

_____

_____

_____

_____

The Philistines blend a pagan worship service with a party celebrating Samson's capture, and they add to their merriment by humiliating him further. But Samson gets an idea, and he turns to the Lord for help (16:28).

✦ Why do you think Samson turns to God for help at this challenging occasion rather than during earlier ones?

....

....

....

....

....

....

....

....

Dagon
The Philistines depended on Dagon, their primary god, for military victory. There was a temple where the Philistines sacrificed to Dagon. This stone idol was carved with the head and torso of a man and the lower body of a fish. Dagon was considered to be a powerful god, and he factored in heavily to how Canaanites, especially the Philistines, lived out their day-to-day lives.[17]

✦ What does Samson's prayer in 16:28 reveal about Samson's motives?

....

....

....

....

....

....

....

✦ Despite Samson's motives, the Lord answers his prayer and empowers Samson to bring down the house and a significant multitude of Philistines. What does this tell us about the Lord and how he works?

....

....

....

....

So ends the story of Samson, the first man raised up by God to fight the Philistines. As the angel had told his mother, Samson *"shall begin* to save Israel from the hand of the Philistines" (13:5). After him would come others to continue the work, most notably the great King David. But the deliverance that came through Samson points to someone even greater than David—the King of kings, Jesus Christ, who would come and deliver God's people from their enemies of sin and Satan.

LET'S TALK

1. The story of Samson actually reflects the story of the entire nation of Israel. They turned to the Lord when personal needs were felt keenly but tended to go their own way and serve themselves much of the time. In reality, this is also our story. Where are you tempted to live like Samson, thinking you're in control of your life and turning to the Lord only when you feel out of control?

2. The power of lust and romantically rooted emotions are put on full display in the story of Samson. There was his marriage to a woman outside the covenant community of God's people. Then there was the hookup with a prostitute. And finally there was his love affair with Delilah. Discuss why such temptations are so powerful. How do we tend to fuel them, and what practical means can we put in place to avoid these temptations? You might want to look at Proverbs 5:1–23 and 1 Corinthians 6:13–20.

NO KING

JUDGES 17:1-18:31

Up until now, we've watched as God raises up one deliverer after the next to rescue his people from the enemy Canaanites. But no longer. The Canaanites fade from view as we see Israel turn even further away from the Lord. We're going to see how abandoning the one true God leads inevitably to destruction. God always intended Israel to dwell safe and secure under his authority, but here again they try to cast him off, rejecting his right to rule over them. They want to live on their own terms, calling their own shots, and the outcome is devastating. It always is when people reject the one true God. We human beings simply weren't created to govern ourselves. We've been hardwired to live under a king. But we'll never submit willingly to a king whom we believe is a tyrant set on forcing us into miserable servitude. That's why the Lord is always at work in the lives of his people to reveal the true King, the one who is a loving, compassionate ruler.

1. MICAH AND HIS MOTHER (17:1-6)

Micah is a thief. That's the first thing we learn about him. He steals a significant amount of silver from his mother and gives it back only because he fears the consequences of a curse.

✦ Micah's mother takes the returned money and has it made into two images to use in worship and gives the images to her son to put in his house. In the process, she dedicates her plan to the Lord. How does Exodus 20:4–5 show that her dedication was misguided?

⬥ Read Isaiah 46:6–7. What does this passage add to our understanding of Micah and his mother?

Micah clearly wants to be a religious man. On his property—likely a compound consisting of several buildings—he erects a shrine and fills it with religious objects, and he even designates one of his own sons as his priest. But there's a problem—God's people were supposed to gather for worship in a specially designated place, not on private property. Plus God's law required that all priests be descended from Aaron the Levite (Exodus 40:12–15), which Micah's family was not.

⬥ How in 17:6 does the narrator of our story assess what Micah does?

2. ALONG COMES A LEVITE (17:7-13)

Back when the land of Canaan was portioned out to the twelve tribes of Israel, the Levites (the descendants from the tribe of Levi set apart as the priests for God's people) were given no land to call their own. Instead the Levites were allotted cities in the midst of other tribes' land. We meet a Levite here who'd been living in Bethlehem, which was part of Judah's territory.

✧ We're told that the Levite left Bethlehem because he wanted to "find a place" (17:8–9). Based on the deal he strikes with Micah, what do you think he was looking to find?

_____

_____

_____

_____

_____

_____

_____

_____

✧ What does Micah believe this arrangement will accomplish for him?

_____

_____

_____

_____

✧ How does Isaiah 1:11–17 shed light on Micah's religious setup? What clues have we been given from Micah's life so far that enable us to make this assessment?

_____

_____

_____

_____

> "*Success is not necessarily a sign of righteousness or an indication that we must be doing something right. It may in fact be the opposite.*"[18]

3. DAN'S DOWNFALL (18:1–31)

Our story broadens out from the life of one man, Micah, to an entire Israelite tribe, Dan. The people of Dan, the Danites, look around at the territories occupied by the other tribes, and they want some of it for themselves. It's not that they'd been left out of the land gift back when Canaan was parceled out to Israel. They had been allotted their own territory, but they'd failed to move in and occupy it (see 1:34). So now, they go on a hunt in the land of Canaan for other land to occupy. As the narrator leads into this section, he reminds us once again that the events he is about to tell occur when there was no king in Israel.

✢ The spies from Dan come to the home of Micah, and there they encounter the Levite priest, whom they recognize, and they ask him to petition God for guidance. They want to know if their land grab will be blessed. In what way is the priest's answer unclear?

Feeling reassured, the Danite spies journey north to a place called Laish, and they like what they see. Citizens of Laish, Canaanite people, seem secure, and they enjoy prosperity, so when the spies bring back this report, the Danites decide this is the place for them. It's worth noting that their motive isn't obedience to God's decree to purge out Canaanite evil. It's the lush landscape that appeals. They want Laish for themselves, and they set out to take it. On their way to Laish, they come once again to the property of Micah, but this time they come six hundred strong, and they plunder Micah's shrine with all its religious objects.

✛ Why does the priest decide to leave Micah's house and go along with the tribe of Dan, and what does this tell us about the motivation of the priest?

_____

_____

_____

_____

_____

_____

A Father's Prophecy

Before the patriarch Jacob died, he foretold what would happen to his twelve sons, who fathered the twelve tribes of Israel. Concerning the descendants of Jacob's son Dan, he prophesied the very incident we read about this week—Dan's unprovoked attack on the city of Laish:

"Dan shall be a serpent in the way,
a viper by the path,
that bites the horse's heels
so that his rider falls backward."
(Genesis 49:17)

✛ We almost feel sorry for Micah as he chases after the Danites and is forced to return home without his possessions. But as we think back to how Micah acquired his shrine and its objects (17:1), how do the following passages shed light on his loss of them?

· Psalm 7:14–16

_____

_____

_____

· Proverbs 26:27

_____

_____

_____

The Danites are successful in their takeover of Laish, and they rename the city Dan. They set up the carved images they'd stolen from Micah along with their own brand of priesthood with the young Levite (whose name we discover is Jonathan).

✦ It seems that the Danites want to worship God but they want to do it in their own way, not bothering to go all the way to the central sanctuary at Shiloh, the only official worship site, to do it. How does Deuteronomy 12:5–14 shed light on why the worship shrine set up at Dan is outside of God's will?

✦ Micah and his mother thought nothing of melting down some silver and making carved images to place in the household shrine. Then the Danites came along and took the carvings and set them up in their own shrine. Why, according to the following passages, was making and setting up such images a dangerous practice?

· Exodus 20:4–6

· Deuteronomy 27:15

· Psalm 97:7

The Tabernacle Tent

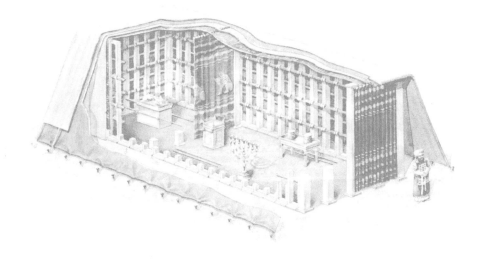

After Israel came into the promised land of Canaan, the tabernacle—a portable temple—was set up at Shiloh.[19]

Micah and the Danites went through the motions of worshiping God, but because they wanted their religious practices to be comfortable and easy, they violated God's stipulations about how and where he wanted to be worshiped. This was a case of worshiping the right God in the wrong way, which, in essence, is a failure to worship God at all.

> *"Micah is living proof that it is possible to be set on a course of religious faith and/or ministry which exudes success in every respect and yet to rest under the curse of God's judgment."*[20]

✦ This week, in the midst of these sad tales of hardened hearts and callous disregard for life, the narrator tells us twice that Israel has no king (17:6; 18:1). What point do you think he is trying to make? Let the passages below shape your answer.

· Psalm 110:1–2

· Jeremiah 23:5–6

· Ezekiel 37:24

· Acts 13:22

· Hebrews 1:8–9

· Revelation 19:11–16

LET'S TALK

1. Misguided worship wasn't a problem only in the days of the judges. Today we aren't as likely to make silver statues and personal shrines, but there are churches that adopt patterns for gathered worship that dishonor the Lord. How can we identify such practices, and what should guide the way we worship?

2. Let's bring this week's lesson to a personal level. When it comes to life in Christ, how are we living out our discipleship? Does the Bible shape your views and govern your day-to-day life? Discuss where and how this is challenging for you and how you can both recognize and avoid compromises.

CRASH AND BURN

JUDGES 19:1-20:48

We come this week to one of the darkest episodes in the history of God's people. Even though it appears here near the end of the book, it actually happened earlier in the judges era. The author of Judges places it here to show us that during this entire era, God's people go from bad to worse. Despite a few threads of gracious hospitality, the story is woven all through with a series of horrors. It begins with a Levite and his concubine. If you recall, a Levite was someone who belonged to the tribe of Levi, the tribe of priests. A concubine was a sort of second-tier wife. This particular Levite and his concubine have reconciled after a four-month separation, and they make their way toward home. Given the length of the journey, they must lodge along the way, so they decide to spend a night in the town of Gibeah in territory belonging to the tribe of Benjamin. We can't help but be shocked as one horror follows another during the night, and the awfulness doesn't end when the new day dawns. The outcome of these few grim hours is war—civil war—as the people of Israel turn on each other.

1. A MATTER OF HOSPITALITY (19:1-21)

We'd never know from this homey opening scene what awaits the Levite and his concubine. Here we find them in the home of her father. In those days—and in some countries today as well—offering hospitality went beyond simple warmth and kindness. It was vitally important. Back then, hosting duties fell primarily to the man as head of the household, and one of those duties was to honor his male guests first and foremost.

✦ Of what does the narrator remind us at the very beginning of this episode?

✦ What do you note about the relationship between the Levite and his concubine in this opening scene?

It seems that the concubine's father does not want his daughter to leave, and, as a good host, he urges the Levite and his daughter to lengthen their stay. Finally, at the end of another day, the Levite determines it's time to go; he won't wait until morning.

✦ They set out toward home and soon come to Jerusalem, which was called Jebus at the time of this incident. Why doesn't the Levite want to spend the night in Jebus?

✦ The travelers come to Gibeah just as the sun is setting and set up for the night in the town square. How in 19:15 is the end of their day set in contrast to its beginning?

....

....

✦ What does the narrator of our story tell us in 19:16 about the identity of the old man who offers the travelers hospitality?

....

....

....

....

2. HEARTS OF DARKNESS (19:22-30)

Watching the scene before us is like streaming an episode from one of those dark Netflix series—pretty disturbing. Here in Judges 19, an evening of delightful hospitality is transformed into a nightmare.

✦ Sadly, this isn't the first time in the Bible this sort of evil has occurred. In the chart below, note the similarities you find between the story here in Judges 19 and the story in Genesis 19.

Sodom (Genesis 19)	Gibeah (Judges 19)
Genesis 19:4-5	Judges 19:22
Genesis 19:6-7	Judges 19:23

Sodom (Genesis 19)	Gibeah (Judges 19)
Genesis 19:8	Judges 19:24
Genesis 19:9	Judges 19:25

The major difference between the episode at Sodom and the one at Gibeah is *who* commits the atrocities. The evil men of Sodom were evil pagans, but the men of Gibeah are God's own people.

✦ What do you think the narrator is trying to tell us from this fact?

....

....

....

....

One of the most painful aspects of this story is how the concubine is treated by men who should be protecting her. As we noted earlier, men were given the highest honor in matters of hospitality, even when it meant sacrificing the well-being of a woman. That's what we see in both stories. Even so, God never intended women to be treated with callous disregard. The fact that it happens in both these incidents is an indication of just how corrupt and far from God those societies had become.

✦ Not only the host but the Levite himself, the concubine's lover, shows no feeling whatsoever toward her suffering. How do the following passages reveal how the Lord wants women and wives to be treated?

· Genesis 2:24

· Deuteronomy 24:5

· Proverbs 5:18–19

· Malachi 2:16

· Ephesians 5:25–29

· 1 Peter 3:7

....

....

....

Naturally the Levite is angry at what happened, but it doesn't seem logical to react by dismembering his concubine and shipping her body parts all over Israel. But he does have a reason. He wants Israel to see just how low the men of Gibeah, from the tribe of Benjamin—brother Israelites—have fallen.

3. ENOUGH IS ENOUGH! (20:1-18)

For the first time in ages, most of Israel unites in a common cause—to punish the evil men of Gibeah who'd attempted an assault on the Levite and then killed his concubine.

🕊 The tribes of Israel strategize their approach to Gibeah, and then they spread out beyond Gibeah to all the territories of Benjamin, men who'd perpetrated the evil attack. How do the people of Benjamin respond in 20:13 to the other tribes' request?

....

....

....

....

🕊 The people of Benjamin take the first step toward full-scale war, mustering troops and special operations forces in preparation to go up against the rest of Israel. Why are the odds stacked against them from the get-go?

....

....

....

....

✣ Before battling Benjamin, Israel turns to the Lord for guidance—something we haven't seen them do for a long time. How does the answer they receive in 20:18 mirror the answer they were given back at the very beginning, in Judges 1:1–2?

✣ The fact that the tribes are guided here the same way they were back in Judges 1:2 actually gives us a hint of light in this otherwise dark story. The specific guidance they receive from the Lord points far into the future. How do Genesis 49:10; Matthew 2:1–6; and Revelation 5:5 enable us to identify this light?

4. BENJAMIN NO MORE (20:19-48)

For the first time in ages, all of Israel is united in a common cause—except for Benjamin. This one tribe *is* the cause. The people of Benjamin have refused to turn over the wicked men of Gibeah for judgment, which makes them just as guilty of evil.

✣ Despite Israel's renewed unity, the war against Benjamin isn't going to be as easy as they'd hoped. After the first hard day of battle, how does Israel prepare for the second day of fighting?

After a second bad day on the battlefield, Israel once again questions the mission, and they seek the Lord's face even more intently. God's people seem to be making a spiritual effort. For one thing, they are fasting and making offerings. Plus the ark of the covenant is here (even though it was supposed to be kept in the tabernacle back in Shiloh). The ark held the tablets on which were inscribed the Ten Commandments. These commandments governed the Lord's special relationship with Israel. We don't want to assume that their efforts were rooted in true zeal for God. In fact, one commentator tells us that Israel had brought the ark to the battle as a "good luck charm."[21] Even so, the presence of Phinehas the high priest is hugely significant. He was the grandson of Moses's brother Aaron, and he had a history for upholding righteousness and purging out evil (see Numbers 25:10–13). Noting the presence of Phinehas, another commentator says: "Theologically speaking, Israel has the means of grace. [The Lord] directs them through his appointed servant, the high priest." Benjamin, on the other hand, "has none of this. No ark, no priest, no direction from [the Lord], no word from heaven, no light in turmoil."[22]

The Ark of the Covenant[23]

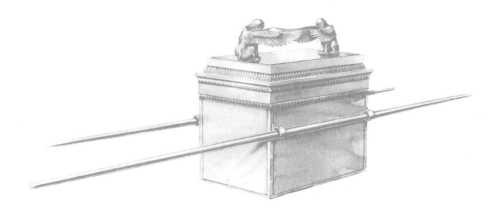

The ark was a wooden chest, overlaid with pure gold, measuring 3.75 feet long, 2.25 feet wide, and 2.25 feet high. It contained within it the two stone tablets of the Testimony (the Ten Commandments). The author of Hebrews adds that it also contained "a golden urn holding the manna, and Aaron's staff that budded" (Hebrews 9:4). The ark was not to be touched by human hands. Two wooden poles, overlaid with gold, were used to transport it and were not to be removed from the ark. The mercy seat, or atonement cover, was a solid golden slab that fitted perfectly on top of the ark. The golden cherubim, which were hammered out of the same piece of gold, had wings outstretched over the mercy seat and faces that looked downward (in reverent awe).

✧ How does the Lord answer Israel's inquiry in 20:28?

....

....

....

....

✧ The battle takes a decisive turn. What does each of the three—the Lord, the people of Israel, and the people of Benjamin—do in 20:35–36?

· The Lord:

....

....

....

· The people of Israel:

....

....

....

· The people of Benjamin:

....

....

....

✧ A carefully planned ambush completes the destruction of Benjamin. Everywhere they turn, they face swords or smoke. There is no escape. Despite their utter defeat, what happens during this chaotic scene to indicate that Benjamin might have a future?

....

....

Anarchy without a King: Bookends of Judges 17–21[24]

Micah and the Danite Migration (chs. 17–18)		Gibeah's Deed and Their Punishment (chs. 19–21)	
Religious Deterioration		Moral Deterioration	
Beginning	"In those days there was no king in Israel. Everyone did what was right in his own eyes" (17:6).	"In those days, when there was no king in Israel . . ." (19:1).	Beginning
Ending	"In those days there was no king in Israel" (18:1).	"In those days there was no king in Israel. Everyone did what was right in his own eyes" (21:25).	Ending

LET'S TALK

1. In the midst of a grim tale, we can't help but find comfort in discovering that God gives grace to undeserving people. We saw it this week in Israel's uniting against evil and then turning to the Lord as they did. We see it in how the Lord was quick to guide them and direct their course to bless them in the long run. As we ponder God's graciousness toward undeserving Israel, how can this encourage us to turn to the Lord even when we've strayed? Israel had the tabernacle, which symbolized God's presence with them, but we have something so much better—the Holy Spirit indwelling us. Talk about grace! When we are overwhelmed with guilt and feelings of shame because of our weaknesses and sins, how can we draw near to God afresh through the means of grace he's made available to us? Consider the place of prayer, the Bible, and your church family. Consider, too, why we don't have to have our spiritual act perfectly together to access these means of grace.

```
........................................................................................
........................................................................................
........................................................................................
........................................................................................
........................................................................................
........................................................................................
```

2. Brother turning against brother—how sad this is! But one way or another, God judges evil, and it's often painful. As Israel fought to purge out the unrepentant men of Benjamin, we see the two-steps-forward-one-back nature of the battle. Isn't that what our own fight against sin is like? Especially those well-entrenched sins, what theologians call "besetting sins." Jesus won the war for his people once for all on the cross, so we've already been delivered from sin's penalty and power. Even so, we will struggle with its presence until we are home in heaven. When it comes to doing battle with our own besetting sins, how do we fight and where is our hope of victory? You might want to include Romans 6:12–14; 8:1–6; Philippians 2:12–13; and 1 John 1:5–10 in your discussion.

```
........................................................................................
........................................................................................
........................................................................................
........................................................................................
........................................................................................
........................................................................................
........................................................................................
```

ROCK BOTTOM

JUDGES 21:1-25

Wait a minute . . . We can't help but experience a moment of confusion when we get to the last chapter in the book of Judges. What is up with Israel? Last week we watched them reunite to go to war against their brother-tribe Benjamin, and after a few setbacks, the Lord granted the united tribes victory. Every man of Benjamin had been annihilated except for six hundred who'd escaped the fray. But now Israel seems to have a change of heart, weeping over the loss of this fellow tribe, and they set out to restore this fallen brother. The plans they make and the means they employ are far from ethical, but through the chaos we once again get glimmers of God's grace.

1. AN OATH REGRETTED (21:1-4)

The war is over, Benjamin defeated, but there are still those six hundred men from Benjamin hiding out in Rimmon. Even so, sooner or later, with no wives and children left, the tribe will just die off. And to ensure the extinction, Israel had vowed that none of their daughters would be allowed to marry one of those lingering Benjaminites.

✦ Israel cries out to the Lord in 21:3. What does their cry indicate about their spiritual understanding at this point?

2. LOOKING FOR LOOPHOLES (21:5–15)

The next day Israel goes through the rituals of worship. They hastily erect an altar for sacrifices—a burnt offering and a peace offering. Burnt offerings were carried out as an act of atonement for sin (Leviticus 1:3–4) and peace offerings symbolized reconciliation and fellowship (Leviticus 17:5). In light of what follows, it seems likely that Israel's offerings were just religious formality. (Genuine faith and love for the Lord show up in what people do when they aren't at a worship service.)

By now, the anger and the heat of battle have cooled, and Israel feels compassion for the surviving six hundred men of Benjamin. They no longer want to see them completely wiped out. At the same time, they are powerless to help because they cannot take back their vow to withhold their daughters from those men. Without those daughters, there won't be any Benjaminite children to rebuild the tribe. But they find a loophole. Some Israelite men from a certain region, Jabesh-gilead, had refused to participate in the war, which meant that their daughters didn't count so far as the vow was concerned.

✛ Capitalizing on this technicality, what does Israel do in 21:10–12?

With celebratory bounty in hand from Jabesh-gilead, Israel invites Benjamin to come home, and a happy reunion takes place. Finally, all twelve tribes are back together again, united in plans and purpose.

✛ What is still lacking for Benjamin at this point?

✦ What is mixed up about Israel's affections and understanding in 21:15?

3. THE DAUGHTERS OF SHILOH (21:16-24)

Despite the women taken by force from Jabesh-gilead, one-third of the Benjaminite men still have no wives. What to do? All the other daughters of Israel must be withheld from Benjamin or their fathers will be cursed. And then another loophole, a way around the vow, comes to light as the annual feast of the Lord, held at Shiloh, draws near.

✦ What is this new plot, and how does Israel explain the loophole to the understandably upset fathers and brothers of Shiloh in 21:22?

✦ What happens to the young women of Shiloh?

4. A KING IS COMING (21:25)

"In those days there was no king in Israel. Everyone did what was right in his own eyes" (21:25). This is the fourth time the narrator has mentioned these two facts (look back at 17:6; 18:1; and 19:1), so they must be important to his story—so important that it's the very last thing he shares.

✦ He wants us to see a connection between these two facts—(1) no king and (2) self-determination. As you reflect on all that's happened in the book of Judges, what connection do you think we are supposed to see?

....

....

....

....

Although Judges ends on this note, Israel is not a lost cause. In fact, despite how hopeless things look, this very last verse is actually a sign of hope. God's people don't yet see that they need a king. They are too caught up in the pride of self-sufficiency to see the harm they're doing not only to their relationship with the Lord but also to their very own lives. They can't recognize yet that what they most need is a king. We humans were never meant to rule ourselves, nor can we. We are just too sinful. All that happens in Judges proves this, and it demonstrates that a king is necessary.

Many more years will pass before Israel faces the reality that their insistence on autonomy will never bless them. Over time, God's people realize that the judges can't save them and that they'd be better off with a king, someone to protect them from the ongoing problems with Canaanite enemies and to provide them materially with social security benefits. So Israel comes to the aging Samuel, the last righteous judge whose story begins in 1 Samuel, and demands a king.

✦ Read the account in 1 Samuel 8:4–7. What do we find out here about what God's people are really seeking?

....

....

....

....

✦ Samuel warns the people that the kind of king they want will prove disastrous, but they won't listen, so the first king of Israel, a man named Saul, is appointed. Sure enough, his reign is a fiasco. Sometimes God gives us what we *want* in order to show us what we really *need*. What a mercy this is! And that's exactly what the Lord does for Israel. What do we learn in the following passages about the king God plans to give Israel?

· 2 Samuel 7:4–17

· Psalm 89:19–29

This king, King David, is the one God has in mind for his people. Israel deserves a tyrant like Saul, but the Lord gives them a righteous ruler like David. This is grace— undeserved favor and blessing. Even more amazing is that David is just a foretaste of the King who will come and bless God's people beyond anything anyone could imagine. Generations later, a descendant of David will rise to the throne. But unlike David, his descendant will never sin against the people he rules or make an unwise leadership decision or act selfishly.

✦ Read Isaiah 9:6–7. What do we learn from Isaiah the prophet about the kind of king God has always intended to give his people?

✦ What more do we learn about this King of kings from the following passages?

 · Luke 1:30–33

....

....

....

 · John 19:16–22

....

....

....

 · 1 Timothy 6:13–16

....

....

....

 · Revelation 17:14

....

....

....

....

Can we see now why the last verse in the book of Judges is actually a sign of hope? And it's saturated with God's grace. After all, the Lord had every right to cut Israel off completely. Not only had they violated the terms of God's covenant—they'd done it again and again, even though God raised up judges to deliver them again and again from messes of their own making. Ultimately, the nation of Israel didn't get the judgment they deserved. Through their failures, the Lord showed them their real need. And ours too, right? Because we really aren't any different from Israel. We love our idols, and we want to live our lives on our own terms. But it doesn't work for us anymore than it did for Israel. Finally God gave them King David, and from King David, he has given all of us King Jesus.

5. A LOOK BACK AT THE JUDGES (HEBREWS 11:32–34)

After our careful study of Israel's judges, we are a bit surprised to see how they are evaluated in the New Testament book of Hebrews. The eleventh chapter of that New Testament letter recounts for us all the Old Testament "heroes" of faith, and that's where we find four of our judges: Gideon, Barak, Samson, and Jephthah. Read Hebrews 11:32–34 and answer the following questions.

✦ To what does the author of Hebrews attribute the judges' heroic acts?

✦ Knowing, as we do, how deeply flawed these judges were, what does their inclusion in the Hebrews "heroes of faith" list reveal to us about how God works to accomplish his purposes?

Hallelujah, the King has come!

> *"This book and the history of the nation that follows serve as eternal testimony to the grim reality that God's people are often their own worst enemy. It is not the enemies outside who threaten the soul but the Canaanite within."*[25]

LET'S TALK

1. As we see in Judges, the spiritual health of a society can be assessed in part by how it treats women and girls. Again this week, we were forced to watch as young women were treated with callous indifference. Women are still treated that way today in many places around the world. Even in our own society, where women have rights and freedoms like never before in history, abuses still occur. For that reason, some of you might know firsthand the damage of abuse. Discuss practical ways to get help, either for yourself or for a woman you suspect might be suffering. Touch on the importance of the church, wise counsel, and godly friendship in that process and in growing in the wisdom to avoid destructive patterns and relationships.

2. God's amazing grace—we need it every bit as much as Israel did in the days of the judges. Like them, we reject God in favor of idols. We've merely replaced Israel's silver statues with the idols of pleasure, beauty, success, and even motherhood. And like Israel, we want to run our own lives rather than do things on God's terms. Describe a time when God rescued you from a mess of your own making and what this taught you about his amazing grace. Or perhaps, right now today, you are struggling and you desperately need to be rescued! If so, how does Hebrews 4:15–16 help you?

3. As we end our study of Judges, summarize what you have learned about:

· the big story of the whole Bible:

· the character of Almighty God:

· salvation in Jesus Christ:

HELPFUL RESOURCES
FOR STUDYING JUDGES

Beale, G. K. *We Become What We Worship: A Biblical Theology of Idolatry*. Downers Grove, IL: IVP Academic, 2008.

Block, Daniel I. *Judges, Ruth*. New American Commentary. Nashville, TN: B&H, 1999.

Davis, Dale Ralph. *Judges: Such a Great Salvation*. Focus on the Bible. Fearn, Ross-shire, UK: Christian Focus, 2000.

Van Pelt, Miles. *Judges: A 12-Week Study*. Knowing the Bible. Edited by J. I. Packer and Dane C. Ortlund. Wheaton, IL: Crossway, 2018.

NOTES

1. "Introduction to Judges," page 435 of the ESV® Study Bible (The Holy Bible, English Standard Version®), copyright © 2008 by Crossway. Used by permission. All rights reserved.
2. George M. Schwab, *Right in Their Own Eyes: The Gospel According to Judges* (Phillipsburg, NJ: P&R, 2011), 16, 20.
3. "The Setting of Judges" map taken from page 434 of the ESV® Study Bible.
4. "The Allotment of the Land" map taken from page 416 of the ESV® Study Bible.
5. "The Judges of Israel" chart taken from page 437 of the ESV® Study Bible.
6. See Ray Vander Laan, "Fertility Cults of Canaan," *That the World May Know* website, accessed October 24, 2020, https://www.thattheworldmayknow.com/fertility-cults-of -canaan. See also ESV® Study Bible, notes on Judges 2:13; 3:7; and 6:25–26.
7. G. K. Beale, *We Become What We Worship: A Biblical Theology of Idolatry* (Downers Grove, IL: IVP Academic, 2008), 307.
8. Beale, *We Become What We Worship*, 307.
9. Daniel I. Block, *Judges, Ruth*, New American Commentary (Nashville, TN: B&H, 1999), 246.
10. Block, *Judges, Ruth*, 246.
11. Dale Ralph Davis, *Judges: Such a Great Salvation*, Focus on the Bible (Fearn, Ross-shire, UK: Christian Focus, 2000), 86.
12. ESV® Study Bible, note on Genesis 16:7.
13. Block, *Judges, Ruth*, 283.
14. Davis, *Judges*, 115.
15. Davis, *Judges*, 126.
16. ESV® Study Bible, note on Judges 11:39.
17. See "Dagon Chief God of the Philistines," *Learn Religions* website, accessed October 26, 2020, https://www.learnreligions.com/dagon-chief-god-of-the-philistines-118505; and J. Mark Bertrand, "What Made Dagon Bow?," accessed October 26, 2020, https://www .cardus.ca/comment/article/what-made-dagon-bow/.
18. Block, *Judges, Ruth*, 514–15.
19. "The Tabernacle Tent" illustration taken from page 186 of the ESV® Study Bible.
20. Davis, *Judges*, 204.
21. Block, *Judges, Ruth*, 561.
22. Davis, *Judges*, 218.
23. "The Ark of the Covenant" illustration and caption taken from page 184 of the ESV® Study Bible.
24. "Anarchy without a King" chart taken from page 467 of the ESV® Study Bible.
25. Block, *Judges, Ruth*, 585.

Also Available in the
Flourish Bible Study Series

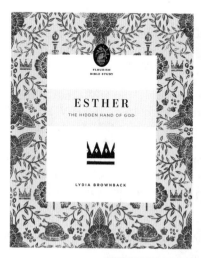

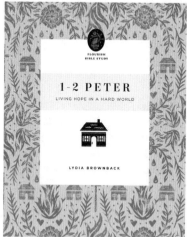

For more information, visit **crossway.org**.